beginnings

an introduction to Christian faith

Director's Manual

Andy Langford and Mark Ralls

Abingdon Press / Nashville

Beginnings: An Introduction to Christian Faith
Director's Manual

Copyright © 2003 by Abingdon Press

Scripture quotations in this publication, unless otherwise indicated, are from the New Revised Standard Version of the Bible, copyrighted © 1989 by the Division of Christian Education of the National Council of the Churches of Christ in the United States of America, and are used by permission.

This book is printed on acid-free, elemental chlorine-free paper.

ISBN 0-687-07339-1

03 04 05 06 07 08 09 10 11 12 — 10 9 8 7 6 5 4 3

MANUFACTURED IN THE UNITED STATES OF AMERICA

Acknowledgments

For the entire *Beginnings* project, Andy Langford and Mark Ralls offer thanks to:

Our fathers: Thomas Anderson Langford, Jr., and Robert Johnson Ralls, pastors, teachers, and leaders in The United Methodist Church, who shared with us the fundamentals of the faith and encouraged the creation of this book.

Our mothers: Ann Marie Daniel Langford and Aileen Fox Ralls, who demonstrated to us how to live as Christians.

Our wives: Sally Lucius Overby Langford and Jennifer Sue Ralls, who patiently listened and encouraged.

A number of clergy of the Western North Carolina Annual Conference who gave impetus to this work. They provided the energy, wisdom, and support to begin this project: Jamie Armstrong, Keith Bingham, Ben Curry, Harley Dickson, Elizabeth Graves, Rodney Hagans, Laurie Hale, Duke Ison, Fred Jordan, Mark Key, Jack Knoespel, Lisa Martinez, Effie McClain, and Ivan Peden.

The members and staff of the following churches in North Carolina who gave us time and support: First United Methodist Church of China Grove, St. Stephen United Methodist Church, Providence United Methodist Church, and St. Timothy United Methodist Church.

Friends who were willing to read various drafts of our work and give us criticism and wisdom: Mark King, Sally Langford, Ann Marie Langford, Dan Hester, Robin Langford, Jamie Armstrong, Elizabeth Graves, Matthew Phillips, Jean Willis, Stephanie Nickell, Lori Langford, and David Renwick.

Members of First United Methodist Church of China Grove and Providence United Methodist Church in Charlotte who heard some of the first drafts of this material and the first class of participants at St. Stephen United Methodist Church in 2001 who endured hearing the first full draft of this resource and offered great insights: Carol, Mabel, Ruddy, Sonia, John, Peggy, Ron, Janet, and Sally.

Contents

Introduction

This book is the resource for pastors, educators, lay leaders, and other persons in local congregations who wish to host *Beginnings: An Introduction to Christian Faith.* This resource is used in conjunction with *Beginnings: Video Resources,* a set of presentations that introduce a Christian response to basic questions of life; *Beginnings: Small-Group Leader's Guide,* a resource for persons who lead discussion groups; *Beginnings: Participant's Guide,* a workbook for program participants; and *Beginnings: Along the Way: A Participant's Companion,* a book that was the foundation of and expands upon the video presentations.

Part One:

Organizing Beginnings:
An Introduction to Christian Faith

In Part One we describe the theological foundations of *Beginnings: An Introduction to Christian Faith,* along with general organizational principles and guidelines. Chapter 1 outlines the general structure and nature of this program. Chapter 2 describes who will participate in it. Chapter 3 discusses the reason for this program: to help persons begin a journey toward Christian faith and life. The next chapters in Part One detail both the general organizational plans and specific requirements that you need to lead this program successfully. Part Two of this book provides you with the necessary planning for each of the two training sessions for those who will lead the program. Part Three offers you detailed guidance to plan and lead the specific, weekly sessions.

1.
Beginnings: The Program

"Evangelism is witness. It is one beggar telling another beggar where to get food. Christians do not offer out of their bounty. They have no bounty. They are simply guests at their Master's table and, as evangelists, they call others too."[1] This quotation by D. T. Niles, a leader of the Methodist Church in Sri Lanka in the first half of the twentieth century, states for us the primary task of the church universal: spiritual beggars sharing gospel food with other spiritual beggars. Our dream is that *Beginnings: An Introduction to Christian Faith* enables you and other followers of Jesus Christ to share an opening course of the gospel feast with inquirers seeking God.

We believe that *Beginnings* is one of the most significant programs you may ever offer in your congregation. Why? We believe this because through this program you invite women and men in your community into a living relationship with Jesus Christ by sharing the basic beliefs of our Christian faith from within your congregation. Through this program, you—pastors, educators, evangelism and outreach leaders, and others in your congregation—can help fulfill the Great Commission given to us by Jesus: "Go therefore and make disciples of all nations, baptizing them in the name of the Father and of the Son and of the Holy Spirit, and teaching them to obey everything that I have commanded you" (Matthew 28:19-20a). The task is great; but as we share the good news, we do so with the confidence that Jesus Christ himself participates in our ministry. As Jesus said, "I am with you always" (Matthew 28:20b). Jesus also offers us the assurance that the kingdom of God has already been established among us and nothing will prevent its ultimate fulfillment. In other words, Jesus Christ is with us on this journey of outreach all the way to the end.

DISTINCTIVE CHARACTERISTICS

Beginnings is a program of the church universal that fulfills our ancient task of sharing the first courses of the gospel feast. This program includes ten distinctive characteristics that make it effective in inviting contemporary inquirers into a living relationship with Jesus Christ within your Christian community:

1. Everyone is welcome. We exclude no one because of lack of knowledge or education, because of membership in a particular group, or because of financial situation or religious background. Throughout *Beginnings,* we honor each participant as a child of God whom God loves and with whom God wants a relationship. As the first disciples on the Day of Pentecost were empowered by the Holy Spirit to speak in languages readily understood, so today *Beginnings* enables you to reach out to everyone and to speak in everyday language.

2. Our program is direct and clear. It avoids esoteric theological language that may confuse newcomers to the church. While the program addresses dozens of the most fundamental theological issues that everyone faces, we use everyday language and illustrations to remove obstacles to a relationship with Jesus Christ. Similar to Philip explaining the gospel to the Ethiopian official as they rode together in a chariot, *Beginnings* helps you meet people where they are.

3. The Bible is our core resource. While we make no attempt to teach the whole of Scripture or to give even an outline of major biblical themes, nevertheless each session is grounded in at least one central biblical narrative that illumines the contemporary lives of participants. *Beginnings* helps you describe the personal, contemporary realities of inquirers within a scriptural framework. By the end of the program, every participant will understand a dozen essential biblical stories that proclaim the heart of the gospel.

4. Our theology is consistent with mainline, Protestant Christianity within the tradition of Christian orthodoxy. We offer a balance between law and gospel, faith and holy living, personal holiness and social holiness, justification and sanctification, grace and works, and evangelicalism and sacramentalism. Holding fast to essential Christian beliefs, we then sit light to all else. We attend strenuously to those beliefs that are genuinely foundational and are relaxed about differences on secondary matters.

5. Our style is one of gracious invitation. We encourage participants to move toward a relationship with Jesus Christ via self-discovery within a loving community rather than via sharp persuasion by an aggressive leader. Women and men need to claim God's grace in their lives and to find Christ at their own pace rather than for us to force them to drink from the living water. Our objective is not to have participants make a decision for Jesus Christ because of an urgent appeal by a charismatic leader but for us to step aside and let Christ gently accompany participants on their own spiritual journeys.

6. Our illustrations are culturally and racially diverse, and our language is inclusive. Voices in this program speak from throughout the centuries of the Christian era and from a variety of Christian traditions. Because the gospel is for all people, irrespective of culture, race, or sex, throughout *Beginnings* we celebrate our God-given diversity.

7. Our program is simple. We do not assume that you must have long, expensive training or advanced theological skills in order to lead this program. *Beginnings* is easy to use and follow. Your congregation should be able to purchase the basic kit, distribute the materials to the right people, make plans efficiently, and then effectively conduct this program.

8. Because following Jesus Christ is not a solitary journey, throughout *Beginnings* we emphasize your congregational setting. For example, we encourage the use of more than one leader from your congregation to enable participants to develop a relationship with your own community of faithful people. Learning in a community of believers establishes deep relationships,

which will support each participant during and after this program. Many people believe that they alone have profound religious questions and that no one has any answers. Participants will discover in this program that everyone has questions and that there are persons in your congregation who have found some answers.

9. *Beginnings* holistically appeals to participants' hearts and heads, feelings and beliefs, emotions and thoughts. We balance intellectually demanding presentations with food, open conversation, and prayer throughout the program. Information is balanced with Christian formation. Our goal is to transform heads, hearts, hands, and feet.

10. Finally, our program fits the lifestyles of newcomers to and new generations in the church. The total program can be completed in as few as nine weeks (with alternative possibilities), requires no additional reading or homework for participants, and involves minimal cost. Additional reading and conversation are available but are not demanded. Yet, in this program you share with participants the heart of the gospel that invites them into a deeper relationship with Jesus Christ.

These ten characteristics make *Beginnings* a wonderful program you can use to offer some filling appetizers in the heavenly banquet to women and men in your community who are searching for God.

SHARING THE FEAST

Although *Beginnings: An Introduction to Christian Faith* is a distinctive program with unique characteristics, it stands in a long line of the theological enterprise of sharing the gospel feast with other people, traditionally entitled "apologetics." Apologetics is the task of explaining the Christian faith to persons outside the bounds of the established church. The very first sermon in Christianity, by Peter in Jerusalem on the Day of Pentecost, was an apologetic defense of Christianity to people who believed that the first disciples were drunk (Acts 2:14-36). Stephen, the first martyr of the church, was stoned to death after witnessing to his faith in Jesus Christ to religious leaders during a trial in Jerusalem (Acts 6–7). Paul preached apologetically before King Agrippa at Caesarea on the coast of the Holy Land (Acts 26). Thus, the universal church of Jesus Christ was established by men and women sharing with other people their walk with Jesus Christ.

Christian writers throughout the following centuries continued this style of theological discourse. Apologists in the first centuries after Jesus, such as Justin Martyr, Origen, and Tertullian, defended their faith in Jesus Christ, repudiated slanderous distortions of their new beliefs, and presented Christianity attractively to their contemporary Greco-Roman culture. These theologians responded to Jews who objected to the idea of Jesus as the Messiah and to pagans who dismissed God's particular revelation in Jesus Christ. These apologists from our distant past defended orthodox Christianity specifically through references to Jesus' miracles, Old Testament prophecies, and the truthfulness of the Bible against heretics, sophists, and skeptics. Throughout the following centuries, especially when Christianity was under duress, apologists such as Augustine, Thomas Aquinas, and John Calvin emerged to teach new cultures the way of Jesus. In this tradition, John Wesley, the English Anglican priest, was an apologist to the social and religious outcasts of eighteenth-century England.

Today, in our post-modern, skeptical, and pluralistic North American culture, we believe that the task of apologetics is needed more than ever. We recognize that new beggars sharing the feast have now appeared throughout the world. Especially in English-speaking societies, modern apologists have arisen who speak to rationalists, secular humanists, and neo-pagans. These apologists include theologians such as the United Methodist Georgia Harkness and the Anglican Michael Green, lay writers such as C. S. Lewis, and popular evangelicals such as Josh McDowell and Anne Graham Lott. We have discovered hundreds of resources, from the book *Christianity: The Basics* (Trinity Press in Australia) to the pamphlet *10 FAQs* (Frequently Asked Questions) (Discipleship Resources in Nashville) to the self-guided study *A Seeker's Guide to Christian Faith* (Upper Room in Nashville) to the workbook *This Is Christianity* (The United Methodist Publishing House in Nashville) to the *Alpha* program (Holy Trinity Brompton in London). These apologetic resources range from historical summaries of the church to simple facts about Christianity to gentle explorations about the connection between personal spirituality and Christian behavior to expansive programs that seek to prove the truthfulness of Christianity.

Beginnings: An Introduction to Christian Faith, among all these resources, is unique in its audience, its approach, and its theology. *Beginnings* is a program for traditional Protestant congregations that enables contemporary Christians to participate in the task of sharing the Christian faith with a new generation of inquirers.

---

1. From "Venite Adoremus II," in *World's Student Christian Federation Prayer Book*; pages 105ff.

2.
Inquirers: The Audience

Our primary mission in *Beginnings: An Introduction to Christian Faith* is to assist you in inviting inquirers into a living relationship with Jesus Christ by sharing the basic beliefs of the Christian faith. Who are these persons? They are the men and women who live next door, work in an adjoining office, eat lunch with you, play on your softball team, exercise with you at the gym, bring their children to your child's birthday party, serve with you on a community board, participate in your supper club, manage your favorite restaurant, come to worship on Christmas Eve, and are part of your extended family. People searching for God, and the people for whom God is searching, are all around us.

SEARCHING STRANGERS

Our North American society is a culture of people looking for meaning. As Henri Nouwen, the late Roman Catholic priest, wrote, "In our world full of strangers, estranged from their own past, culture and country, from their neighbors, friends, and family, from their deepest self and their God, we witness a painful search for a hospitable place where life can be lived without fear and where community can be found."[1] In this culture of searching strangers, many persons in our society are looking for "something." As described by religious sociologists and theologians, "there are many people on a spiritual quest, cobbling together their faith from a patchwork quilt of a little this and a little that, a nation full of people who want the benefits of adherence to a religious tradition with none of the limits."[2] Our program aids you in assisting the spiritual quest of such searching strangers.

In the broadest sense, every one of us is an inquirer.

Part of our human condition is to ask questions of ourselves, of one another, and of God. But in this program we are even more specific. That is, we are specifically interested in those persons outside the institutional church who are intentionally asking questions about the meaning of life as experienced by Christians. Inquirers are also the new believers and new church members in your congregation. These latter persons have just come into your community and are asking profound questions. Both sets of these inquirers are on a quest to discover whether the God of the Old and New Testaments can give meaning and direction to their own lives and to the whole world. This program responds to the fundamental questions these searching people ask most.

In addition, we focus on adults in North America who are between twenty-five and forty-five years of age. These women and men are asking profound questions about the meaning, direction, and purpose of their lives and of our society. This generation of searchers also represents the largest number of persons in the United States who do not participate in any organized religion. *Beginnings* encourages these adults in your community toward a relationship with Jesus Christ and participation in your congregation.

In traditional language, *Beginnings* serves primarily as a pre-baptismal catechesis, teaching adults preparing for baptism. In parts of the early church, that process took three years and was led by Christian believers within the congregation who shared with people who were considering following Jesus Christ. *Beginnings* provides for Christian leaders inside the church, like you, a gentle and inviting introduction to the Christian journey for searching strangers.

These inquirers fall into four major groups:

non-Christians, often called seekers; unchurched but cultural Christians; new believers in Jesus Christ; and new members of your congregation.

INQUIRERS BEYOND THE CHURCH: SEEKERS AND CULTURAL CHRISTIANS

The first two groups of inquirers, our primary audience, are those men and women who are not a part of an established Christian or other faith community and yet are on a profound spiritual journey.

The first group, we call them seekers, know very little about Jesus Christ and have never participated in a Christian community. They grew up in homes and communities where religion was rarely discussed and faith was not practiced. Yet, today these seekers are asking serious, fundamental questions regarding their lives and simply do not know whom to ask. These persons are truly beyond the bounds of the established church, but they are certainly not beyond your ability to reach and certainly not beyond the bounds of God's grace.

The second group, called the unchurched, we sometimes name as "cultural Christians." These inquirers possess some basic knowledge about Jesus Christ—knowing, for example, that Christmas celebrates the birth of Jesus. They also may occasionally participate in Christian worship services such as weddings, funerals, or Christmas Eve services. These cultural Christians consider themselves to be Christian, but they know little about the content of orthodox Christianity and have not adopted the practices of discipleship. They believe themselves to be Christian because Christianity has been the dominant social and ethical culture of North America for the past four hundred years.

These first two groups of inquirers are our major audience. These seekers and cultural Christians, based on various surveys, number approximately one hundred million people in the United States. While almost two thirds of these inquirers believe themselves to be nominal Christians or moderately committed Christians—they say that they "believe in God"—they rarely exhibit lifestyles that reflect a strong relationship with Jesus Christ. While some of these men and women occasionally read the Bible and pray, they stand outside any organized community of faith. These persons are spiritual without any specific connection with a religious community like yours.

None of the people in these first two categories identify themselves as committed atheists/agnostics (Only about ten percent of the United States population professes to have no belief in God.) or are actively committed to other religious traditions (Persons who claim Judaism, Mormonism, Islam, Hinduism, Buddhism, Sikhism, or other faiths as their spiritual home now number about ten percent of the population of the United States.). We recognize that the United States of America today is the most religiously diverse nation on the planet.[3] While we understand that some atheists and believers of other religions may attend *Beginnings* and that it is our responsibility to share our faith clearly and unambiguously, the redirection of people away from their own established faiths to Christianity is not our primary aim. Our goal is not to put down or to bear false witness against other faiths but to witness to and share our Christian faith. We Christians can be both committed to our Christian faith and tolerant of those persons who are not.

Many seekers and cultural Christians experience a deep need for a relationship with God and a community of faithful people like yours. These people are truly spiritual; but often they are not comfortable with organized religion, as they understand it. They suffer all the ills of human life that also afflict faithful Christian believers—divorce, physical illness, mental illness, broken relationships, grief, work difficulties, financial problems—but they are not certain about where to find answers to their questions about these matters.

Like all persons everywhere, they have basic primary needs: how to establish strong personal relationships, be physically and emotionally healthy, manage money, rear children, be compassionate, find meaning in their lives, and be part of a community. *Beginnings* assists you in reaching out first and foremost to these seekers and cultural Christians.

CHRISTIAN INQUIRERS: NEW BELIEVERS AND NEW MEMBERS

In addition to seekers and cultural Christians, there are two additional groups of inquirers who will benefit from participation in *Beginnings*: new Christian believers and new members of your congregation.

New believers are the third set of persons who will be attracted to this program. These people have begun to know Jesus Christ as Savior, but they may be uncertain about the basic beliefs of Christianity. They are just beginning an intentional walk with Jesus Christ. These women and men are just starting to practice discipleship and are making tentative steps toward being a part of your covenant community. Some of these people may want to participate in *Beginnings* as a basic introduction to their newfound faith.

New members of your congregation are the final set of participants who will find *Beginnings* attractive. These persons are the believers in Jesus Christ who have publicly committed to live out their faith in your local church community. While some of these persons have been lifelong Christians and know the basic theological beliefs of Christianity, many other new church members have been away from the Christian faith for an extended period of time and are not certain about our basic beliefs. In many cases, their children are asking profound questions; and they do not have any answers. In addition, they still have questions about how Christians are supposed to live. For these people, *Beginnings* provides a basic introduction to the beliefs and practices held in common by most Protestant Christians in congregations like yours.

These four groups of persons—seekers, cultural Christians, new believers, and new church members—are the primary audience for this program.

CHURCHED BELIEVERS

But what about your established church members? Are faithful followers of Jesus Christ not inquirers also? Longtime believers and members of your congregation often ask questions about the basic beliefs and practices of Christianity. Unlike the above groups of persons, however, these saints are well along on their journey to Christian maturity; they need meat, not milk. Their theological questions are often more nuanced, and they often wish to discuss specific Christian doctrines. Some of these more mature believers who participate in this program may complain to you that *Beginnings* is too simple or too basic for them. These established Christians are absolutely correct. Mature Christians have already wrestled with these basic questions and have come to

some conclusion about how Christians answer them. Because your congregation has been faithful in its ministry of preaching and teaching, this program simply reinforces your members' existing knowledge. For persons who want to know more and to grow in serious discipleship, you may offer other courses and programs such as DISCIPLE BIBLE STUDY, *Companions in Christ*, *Witness*, *Kerygma*, CHRISTIAN BELIEVER, and JESUS IN THE GOSPELS. These programs and other ministries like them provide substantially more theological and biblical content and have very specific expectations of participants. They are typically more appropriate for your faithful saints to grow in grace.

BELIEVERS SHARING WITH SEEKERS

What then is the role of your established believers in Jesus Christ in this program? *Beginnings: An Introduction to Christian Faith* encourages your established Christian believers to participate by inviting their friends, family, and neighbors who are outside or new to the church to come with them and discuss the basic questions of life within your congregation.

You may want to invite a group of longtime members to participate as a way to begin this program. It can serve as a helpful refresher course for many who sit in the pews, Sunday after Sunday, and still yearn to know more about the gospel. Some of these people simply may not understand the basic beliefs of the gospel. In the words of John Wesley, they may be "half-way Christians." *Beginnings* reminds these women and men anew about the first courses of the gospel banquet.

Beginnings can help seasoned Christians understand the distinctive characteristics of Christianity and then give them confidence to consider sharing their faith with people who are not now following Jesus Christ or who have just begun the journey. They are the ones who will invite their unchurched friends, family members, neighbors, and coworkers to attend the program the next time it is offered. Many of the clergy and staff of local congregations have very little contact with non-Christians and cultural Christians; but all church members live, work, and play next to people outside the church every day. We want to help your members notice the unchurched, engage in a relationship with them, invite them as guests to this program, and demonstrate the role of Jesus Christ in the life of your active community of faith. Our goal is to help you create a congregational culture in which your members become apologists to every serious inquirer by their words and actions. We are assisting faithful Christian believers in creating space in which new inquirers may claim God's grace in their lives.

---

1. From *Reaching Out,* by Henri Nouwen (Doubleday, 1975); page 65.

2. From *Conversion in the Wesleyan Tradition,* by Will Willimon (Abingdon, 2000); page 243.

3. See *A New Religious America*, by Diana Eck (HarperSan Francisco, 2001) for evidence of this diversity.

3.
Redirection: The Goal

Our goal in *Beginnings: An Introduction to Christian Faith* is to redirect women and men toward the way of Jesus Christ. By the power of the Holy Spirit, through this program you and your congregation may point women and men toward a deep and lifelong relationship with Jesus Christ. In biblical language, as John the Baptist proclaimed, our task is to help "make straight the way of the Lord" (John 1:23) in order that people may begin to understand that Jesus is "the way, and the truth, and the life" (John 14:6).[1] We invite people to come to God's feast, believing Jesus when he said, "I have come that you might have life, and have life abundantly" (John 10:10).

REDIRECTION AND CONVERSION

"We cannot forget the power of Christian conversion, that radical decision to turn away from sin and back to God, which reaches to the depths of a person's soul and can work extraordinary change."
Pope John Paul II

"Redirection" is our word for the first steps in conversion. Conversion is God's gift of grace that enables persons to turn around, move from one set of relationships to another set of relationships, reject evil and affirm goodness, make a U-turn, shift 180 degrees, follow in the steps of Jesus, and start anew. Because we believe that conversion is a lifelong journey that encompasses the whole of a person's life, we do not believe that anyone will enter into a holistic relationship with Jesus Christ simply by participating in *Beginnings*. We do believe, however, that through this program many women and men are given the opportunity to choose intentionally a new direction to travel that ultimately will lead them to an abundant life in Jesus Christ.

This new life in Christ begins with a call from God, is furthered when an individual responds, and then moves toward completion for the rest of her or his life. As Jesus said to Nicodemus, "No one can see the kingdom of God without being born from above" (John 3:3). One classic description of the first step of conversion occurred in the life of the Pharisee Saul (a man we know as the apostle Paul), after his experience on the road to Damascus (Acts 9). Paul, a persecutor of the followers of Jesus, upon seeing a bright light and hearing the voice of Jesus Christ, began his change into a preeminent proclaimer of the gospel.

The first steps of most Christians are not like Paul's, however. From the first followers of Jesus to every follower of Christ today, every conversion begins differently and develops in multiple ways. Indeed, each conversion is unique; no one pattern fits everyone. In all cases God's work is primary; our human response is secondary. Conversions may be dramatic and/or subtle, emotional and/or intellectual, exciting and/or plain, instantaneous and/or gradual, personal and/or corporate, the result of a single precipitating crisis and/or a gradual process of becoming, or a combination of all the above. Conversion involves a constellation of many factors, with multiple moments and configurations.

All conversions, however, require an environment and a process that encourage such a newfound relationship. From a bright light on the road to Damascus to reading a book in a garden to a sudden revelation in a private room to the study of Scripture to a prayer meeting to a late night experience, every moment of redirection or conversion takes place in a particular setting. We hope that *Beginnings* can be such a setting in your congregation. In addition, while a conversion may occur in any environment in the twinkling of an eye, spiritual transformation is always part of a process that has a beginning and points toward a goal. Contemporary studies by theologians such as James Fowler in *The Stages of Faith* provide empirical, psychological support for understanding conversion as process. Jesus used the expression (found in John 3:3) "born from above" (NRSV) or "born anew" (RSV) or "born over again" (NEB) or "born again" (KJV) to describe the beginning of a spiritual life. John Wesley added a more developmental understanding of conversion as "a thorough change of heart and life from sin to holiness."[2] The New Testament speaks about becoming a child of God and then maturing in the faith. While the birth of a child is a foundational event, the life that follows any birth is even more exciting and rich. The Bible uses many images to represent spiritual growth from birth to maturity: growing wheat, constructing a house, or going on a journey. All these images involve both a place and a process of development, both of which you can provide through this program.

"We are to preach *metanoia*. We must entice people away from the world to God." Hans Küng

Conversion, thus, is an experience that encompasses the whole of human life. The first steps of conversions may begin in this program, but they will continue for the rest of the participants' lives.

The program is intellectually honest and demanding. Just as Paul presented Christ to rational skeptics in Athens, through this program you offer the truth of Christianity as intellectually sound. You share biblical stories and personal statements of belief so that participants need not take irrational leaps or be asked to accept simplistic understandings of Christianity. Instead, people may take some first steps of faith based on a clear understanding of the essential beliefs of orthodox Christianity.

Because trust is needed as well, *Beginnings* also reaches for the heart. The gospel does not just require intellectual agreement with a set of biblical principles; rather, it calls men and women to fall in love with Jesus Christ in a way that engages all of their heart and soul. By appealing to both the head and the heart, you encour-

age everyone to begin to respond to the invitation by Jesus, "Come to me, all you that are weary and are carrying heavy burdens, and I will give you rest" (Matthew 11:28). When the head and heart are bridged, your participants' hands and feet will follow; and their lives will begin to resemble the example of Jesus. In other words, *Beginnings* assists you in inviting all inquirers to make a decision to begin the journey of being a disciple of Jesus Christ and then to continue that journey throughout their lives.

Even at the beginning of this process, conversion must be understood not only to involve individuals but also the whole of creation. A primary misunderstanding among some people is that God's transformation is individualistic and even narcissistic—all that matters is "Jesus and me." The gospel declares, however, that God through the Holy Spirit is doing a new thing, creating a new kingdom, and establishing a new day, of which individual conversions are only a part. Salvation is about what God does in and for each person and in and for the whole universe. God's new realm challenges individuals and every culture, especially our North American society, to work toward fundamental realignment with the reign of God. While we Christians may talk about how Jesus Christ affects an individual's life, this personal relationship can be fully understood only in light of the larger and more radical movement of God to redeem all creation. As Will Willimon writes, "Conversion, being born again, transformed, regenerated, detoxified, is merely God's means of getting God's way with the world."[3] Through *Beginnings* you invite people to consider becoming disciples who will ultimately participate fully in this new kingdom.

THE FIRST STEPS TOWARD REDIRECTION

Successfully inviting persons into a living relationship with Jesus Christ in your community of faith does not happen overnight but comes by taking a number of initial steps along the way. As people participate in this program, we believe that all of the following initial steps are possible and may well happen when your community of faith shares its holy banquet with others:

1. Wherever your inquirers are in their walk with God, they may acknowledge or have awakened in

them a hunger for Jesus Christ. By identifying this hunger, which all inquirers possess, *Beginnings* helps each participant experience the presence of God as revealed in Scripture and in your Christian community.

2. Participants may begin an intentional spiritual journey. Every inquirer is in a sense already on a journey with God; this is why these persons are taking part in the program with you. The goal of *Beginnings* is not for participants to complete the sessions and receive a certificate from you to frame and place on a wall. Rather, this program offers specific suggestions for inquirers to begin an intentional and disciplined relationship with Jesus Christ that will continue for the rest of their lives.

3. Participants may begin to understand the relevance of Christianity to modern life. Many persons both inside and outside the church do not believe that Christianity speaks to the real issues in their lives, adds value to their existence, and influences culture. Many times people only understand a caricature of Christianity, however, not the true faith. At the end of this program, some people may still find Christianity irrelevant to their lives; but if they do, at least they will be basing their decision on what Christianity is really all about, rather than on a distorted picture of it. *Beginnings* provides your participants with a clear, biblical overview of the essential beliefs and practices of the Christian life.

4. Participants practice briefly some of the basic ways Christians experience God: through fellowship with other Christians, possibly hearing or singing Christian music, Bible study, Christian testimonies, and prayer. *Beginnings: An Introduction to Christian Faith* is not a dinner club, worship service, systematic Bible study, or prayer group. Yet, all of these elements are part of the whole. By the end of the program, inquirers will be comfortable socializing with Christians, learning biblical stories, watching how other people experience Jesus Christ, sharing deep concerns, and praying together.

5. All participants have space and opportunity to respond to the gospel. While we do not encourage you to pressure anyone to have an identifiable conversion experience, throughout the program God may call participants to respond positively to Jesus Christ's love for them. It is not enough just to know the basics of the gospel; eventually an inquirer must either respond to

Jesus' invitation with a "yes" or "no." In this program, we provide the opportunity for participants to respond. See especially the section at the end of Chapter 7 for a discussion about "How Can I Begin an Intentional Journey With Jesus Christ?"

6. Finally, participants who are not members of your congregation may consider church membership. *Beginnings* does not force non-Christians or unchurched participants to join your congregation, but we do offer reasons to participate in your community of faith. *Beginnings* is not first and foremost a congregational membership class. Such a membership class, we believe, should include specific content about the mission, ministries, and history of your congregation. Rather, *Beginnings* is more basic. The program invites persons to consider having a continuing relationship with Jesus Christ in community with other people in your congregation who are already in relationship with God. After completing the program, many participants may join your congregation; but an introductory personal relationship with Jesus Christ is the more basic objective.

The decisions that participants make should be acts of free will and not responses to pressure to continue going in the direction this program leads. We should not endlessly exhort any participant to respond positively, and we should not run after people if they do not. God alone converts. We who lead *Beginnings* only witness and invite persons to the feast. People must make their own decisions. Over the period of a few short weeks, as the Holy Spirit works in people's hearts, they will make the decisions appropriate for them in their walk and relationship with God.

When inquirers gather in your community of faith as you offer them *Beginnings*, all of these first steps are possible; and their journey with Jesus Christ is well underway.

CONGREGATIONAL EVANGELISM

At this point, we hope that it is clear why we believe that *Beginnings* should be grounded in a local congregation. The place where Jesus Christ's ministry of invitation to new life connects with contemporary inquirers is in your local congregation of faithful followers. We agree with William Barclay that "there ought to be a much closer connexion between conversion and the church. It is the strange and odd fact that as things now are it is not in the Church that we expect to find conversions happening. We have actually come to a state of things when we expect to find conversions happening at missions and campaigns outside the Church rather than within the ordinary work, ministry, and activity of the Church. . . . Conversion will never be what it was meant to be until it happens within the Church, and the Church will never be what it was meant to be until each who enters it makes a conscious and deliberate decision."[4]

Evangelism, sharing the good news of Jesus Christ with a hungry world, is both a personal opportunity for individual believers and even more so a corporate obligation of every congregation. Every member of your congregation can be a midwife to persons being born in Christ, and your congregation itself can provide the birthing room. In other words, every member of your congregation can be a spiritual guide; and your congregation can be the place of spiritual formation. Just as the medieval poet Dante was led by his guides Virgil and Beatrice from the inferno to paradise in *The Divine Comedy*, so too the participants in this program may be guided by those in your congregation who are able to give spiritual direction. Individual Christians who have experienced the love of Jesus Christ have an enthusiasm for sharing the good news. And individual witness about Christ by a follower of Jesus is given best by those who are active members of a community of faith.

As a means of inviting people to consider the possibility of redirection, *Beginnings* is an example of what Robert Webber calls "postmodern evangelism." It promotes "a communal atmosphere of embodied faith, an awakening of faith in a healthy community of believers."[5] You are providing participants with the opportunity to think, watch, and listen and to talk through their questions and difficulties, in other words, to let the initial steps of redirection toward conversion unfold.

At its heart, *Beginnings* enables all the participants to trust one another and God in Jesus Christ so that a relationship with Christ may flourish. Many inquirers will arrive feeling skeptical, fearful, anxious, cynical, and distrustful toward the established church and our Savior. They may wonder if you and your congregation are after their money, their mind, or something else. For example, the number one reason persons say they stay away from

organized religion is that they fear it only wants their money. This is why we suggest that your congregation offer the entire program without cost to participants who are not members of your congregation. Building a level of trust will take weeks, probably months. *Beginnings* is simply the first course of the feast and the first few steps. But in these first steps, as participants who are not members of your congregation become friends with persons in their small group who are, they will begin to see that people in your congregation truly care about them as individuals. They will recognize that what the church offers, the good news of Jesus Christ, is fundamentally free.

Lone evangelists seldom succeed in carrying out the Great Commission. The church's greatest evangelists, from Augustine in Hippo to Wesley in England to Billy Graham in the United States, all created simple yet profound ministries that surrounded potential Christians with strong communities of faith. In this tradition, there are several reasons why we base our program in your local congregation:

1. Inquirers will experience your living community of faith. Through participating in *Beginnings,* persons become familiar with the setting, the people, and the culture of your particular community of faithful Christians. While most congregations exhibit many characteristics in common with other congregations, every congregation is unique; each congregation has its own ethos, emphases, and culture. Once a participant who is not a member of your church gets to know your congregation and some of its members, he or she will be much more likely to stay. In today's culture, people belong, then believe, and then join. Some people visit a congregation for years prior to joining it. *Beginnings* is a first step into Christian community.

2. *Beginnings* has the potential to involve everyone in your congregation in the task of evangelism. In your congregation there are people who have diverse gifts that can be used in a holistic ministry of evangelism, but often their gifts are not recognized or used. For example, while many members understand that sharing the gospel is both an obligation and an opportunity, only a few Christians ever participate in evangelism. Most church members are often uncertain what to do and believe they do not have the knowledge or skills necessary. *Beginnings* requires the involvement of many believers throughout your congregation, from preparing a hospitable space to greeting people at the door to fixing a meal to leading music to sharing financially to leading a small group. In addition, everyone in your congregation may participate in *Beginnings* by undergirding your program with prayer.

3. Many seemingly faithful people in your congregation, by their participation in this program, may also grow in their relationship with Jesus Christ. As E. Stanley Jones, the great Methodist evangelist from the middle of the twentieth century, wrote, "The acid test of the validity of a Christian Church is whether it can not only convert people from the outside to membership but also produce conversion within its own membership. When the church cannot do both, it is on its way out."[6] Your longtime members may be changed by their involvement in facilitating the spiritual growth of new people. The fact that established Christians may grow as a result of helping with the program is one reason your longtime members need to be as involved as seekers, cultural Christians, new believers, and new members.

4. The success of *Beginnings* depends on one essential element that requires your congregational members to participate: friends inviting friends. *Beginnings* follows the New Testament model of evangelism: Simon Peter invited his brother Andrew to meet Jesus; Philip brought his friend Nathanael; friends lowered a paralyzed friend down to Jesus; the woman at the well introduced Jesus to everyone in her town; Matthew held a feast and invited his colleagues to meet Jesus; and Lydia in Macedonia invited Paul to preach the gospel in her home and throughout Europe. Today, the vast majority of people come to Jesus Christ not because of a pastoral visit or a television ad or a four-color brochure, but through the invitation of a trusted friend, family member, or colleague.

Beginnings encourages your church members to invite their friends, neighbors, coworkers, and families to come to a meal, share friendly conversation, listen to and watch a video/DVD, and discuss their questions. When these persons begin to know Jesus Christ and recognize the role of God in their lives, they will then want to tell their friends, family members, and coworkers. These friends of the first participants, once they have experienced *Beginnings*, will in turn invite their friends, family members, and coworkers to a subsequent program.

Like a stone thrown into a pond, the circle of influence grows.

When members of your congregation offer invitations to their friends to meet Jesus Christ, good things will happen. A major community crusade may bring great blessings to persons and a community; but such major revivals can be limited, and the results often dissipate over time. Individual, one-on-one faith sharing is also valuable; but only a few people have such holy boldness, and only a few persons may be reached by any one person. Our hope is that every congregation will offer an effective, ongoing program of local church evangelism such as *Beginnings*. Every congregation, whether large or small, rural or urban, rich or poor, has a responsibility to offer Jesus Christ to each child, youth, and adult. As the mission statement of The United Methodist Church declares, the task of every congregation is "to make disciples of Jesus Christ." If every congregation offered such a program—friends inviting friends inviting friends—how quickly the gospel would be shared!

5. The program's location in your local church assures that salvation is ultimately not an individual affair but a community experience. When someone becomes a new person in Christ, she or he must necessarily become a part of a living body of other believers. As the early church grew by its members sharing in prayer, breaking bread together, and sharing resources, so new followers of the Way must become a part of the body of Christ. This communal quality of salvation is why one of the final sessions is on church membership. Congregational evangelism through *Beginnings* will assist persons in taking the first steps in their journey with Jesus Christ.

SUMMARY

Michael Green, an evangelist in the Church of England and professor at Cambridge University, writes why a program such as *Beginnings* will be successful in helping persons take these first steps: "Whenever Christianity has been at its most healthy, evangelism has stemmed from the local church, and has had a noticeable impact on the surrounding area. I do not believe that the re-Christianization of the West can take place without the renewal of local churches in this whole area of evangelism. We need a thoughtful, sustained, relevant presentation of the Christian faith, in word and in action, embodied in a warm, prayerful, lively local church which has a real concern for its community at all levels. . . . Such evangelism, in and from the local church, is not only much needed but . . . eminently possible. I believe it to be the most natural, long-lasting and effective evangelism that is open to us."[7]

Or, as Robert Webber, an evangelical Episcopalian, writes, "An effective evangelism must simultaneously encourage Christian people to share their story of faith with neighbor and friend and create the inquiry as a formal way of dealing with people who are genuinely interested in converting to Christ. Active church members will be more likely to do initial evangelism if there is a support community in the church to carry converts through the various stages of conversion. To bring a person who shows interest in the gospel into a church that has no ordered mean of organizing and deepening his or her experience with Christ is self-defeating."[8]

Beginnings may be one of the most exciting programs ever presented in your congregation. As your congregation participates in the historic task of apologetics, the gospel is proclaimed, new persons are offered a relationship with Jesus Christ, and the church fulfills its com-

mission. During this program all participants will be invited to redirect their lives toward the way of Jesus Christ and the heavenly banquet. Thanks be to God!

1. See *The Mystery and Meaning of Christian Conversion*, by George Morris and other resources listed in Chapter 8. Additional Resources for a fuller discussion of conversion.

2. From *The Complete English Dictionary*, 3rd edition, by John Wesley (Hawes, 1777).

3. From *Conversion in the Wesleyan Tradition*, by Will Willimon (Abingdon, 2001); page 22.

4. From *Turning to God*, by William Barclay (Baker Bookhouse, 1973); pages 102–103.

5. From *Celebrating Our Faith: Evangelism Through Worship*, by Robert Webber (Harper & Row, 1986).

6. From *Conversion,* by E. Stanley Jones (Abingdon Press, 1959); page 27.

7. From *Evangelism Through the Local Church,* by Michael Green (Thomas Nelson, 1992); pages ix–x.

8. From *Celebrating Our Faith: Evangelism Through Worship*, by Robert Webber; page 10.

4.
Organization: Setting Up the Program

Your leadership of *Beginnings: An Introduction to Christian Faith* demands a serious effort by you and your congregation; but when you share the tasks, the whole experience becomes enjoyable for everyone. The following sections in this chapter explain how you can plan and lead this program. Later chapters are dedicated to specific requirements for key leaders and their responsibilities (Chapter 5), weekly sessions (Chapter 6), and small groups (Chapter 7). Also included are resources for additional reading (Chapter 8), copies of forms that you may duplicate for the program (Chapter 9), and suggestions for meals (Chapter 10).

RESOURCES

There are five basic resources that make up *Beginnings: An Introduction to Christian Faith*:

Beginnings: Director's Manual, this book, is the resource for you—pastors, educators, evangelistic lay leaders, and other persons in your local congregation—who are the lead hosts of the program. In this book we have provided the theological background to this program and basic information needed to conduct *Beginnings* in your congregation. One copy per congregation may be sufficient, although additional copies may be helpful to assist the major leaders of your program.

Beginnings: Video Resources is a series of twelve video/DCD presentations (each approximately fifteen minutes in length) about the basics of Christianity. This audiovisual resource provides the basic content for each session. Only one copy is required for your congregation.

Beginnings: Small-Group Leader's Guide is the resource for the persons in your congregation who guide the small-group discussions following the video/DVD presentation; it also has useful information for all the other members of your leadership team. This book contains basic background information, suggestions on how to lead a group for spiritual formation, and specific guidance for each session. The basic content of each of the two training sessions, for example, is included in outline form in this resource. Each of your small-group leaders and the director should have their own copy of this resource.

Beginnings: Participant's Guide is the workbook for participants. This workbook follows the outline of the video/DVD presentations and may be used as a journal for note taking and further reflection. Each participant will need to receive his or her own copy at the start of the program. We suggest that your congregation provide this book at no cost to the participants who are not members of your congregation, since they are your guests.

Beginnings: Along the Way: A Participant's Companion is an engaging book that parallels and complements *Beginnings: Video Resources*. Most of your congregational hosts and many guests may wish to purchase the book (or give them a copy) to continue their study of a particular issue and question. This book provides the core biblical story, additional Scripture references, and supplemental illustrations that were the basis for the video presentation and expand upon the basic presentations. You, the *Beginnings* director, may find it very helpful to review this text as the foundation for the basic content portion of the program and then present the material orally—adapted, of course, by you for your particular audience.

Each participant needs a Bible throughout the program. While there are more Bibles in the United States than people, many people still own only a King James Version. These same people also believe that the Bible is hard to read and difficult to understand. When your congregation hosts *Beginnings*, you may find it quite helpful to make available to each participant a copy of a version of the Bible that is easy to read. These Bibles may also be given without charge to participants who are not members of your congregation. While *Beginnings: Participant's Guide* contains the primary biblical text for each session, there are a number of other references that are not printed, which your participants may wish to review. We recommend the New Revised Standard Version or the New International Version or another contemporary translation.

A short promotional video is included with the video resources to help you promote *Beginnings* both inside and outside your congregation. Please view the video before using, to make sure it is appropriate to your needs.

KEY ELEMENTS

Beginnings has a number of key elements that are part of each session of the program. Each of these foundational elements is essential for participants to have a positive experience:

1. Inviting. Anyone interested in discovering more about the Christian faith is invited. All four key audiences—seekers, cultural Christians, new believers, and new members—may attend and experience *Beginnings*, along with your faithful saints, and enjoy the program.

2. Eating. Sharing a meal together gives everyone the chance to know one another and to develop Christian friendships. Just as Jesus ate with saints and sinners in settings ranging from wedding parties to bread and fish beside the Sea of Galilee to a Passover meal, so at each session the participants eat together in a hospitable setting prior to any serious discussion. The food does not have to be elaborate or expensive, but eating together builds community. A wide variety of meal suggestions are provided in Chapter 10. Meals.

3. Laughing. We encourage you to create an environment that is relaxed and welcoming. Laughing, acknowledging mistakes, and creating a fun environment help break down barriers and enable everyone to relax. Be careful, however, about jokes. Jokes should never pick on any individual or make fun of a particular group.

4. Singing and worshiping. Each session offers you the possibility of a short period of music. The intent of the music is to help participants relax, not to teach them how to sing hymns or Christian music. Especially if you have some talented musicians and singers in your congregation, invite them to attend and share their gift of music. Be careful, however; this is not the time to teach people about Christian worship. Warm hospitality, not teaching, is the key. In the later weeks of the program, we will offer the possibility of Holy Communion (during the Day Apart retreat) and a Love Feast (during the final session.)

5. Learning. The program consists of twelve video/DVD presentations in which Rob presents the core of the Christian faith. Participants are eager to learn about the Christian faith and to consider how the gospel speaks to their own lives. These video/DVD presentations address the most profound questions that inquirers ask and present the basic elements of Christian belief in engaging ways.

6. Asking. *Beginnings* encourages all the participants to understand that no question or reaction is too simple, too hostile, or too odd. After the video/DVD presentation, your small-group leaders will encourage participants to discuss the presentation and to ask questions. The only bad questions are those that are not asked.

7. Sharing. In the small-group discussions that follow each video/DVD presentation, everyone takes part and supports the other participants along the way. This is the time for good, deep conversation. Honest dialogue leads persons to an honest relationship with God. During the small-group discussions, participants share about themselves and care for one another. Persons from your congregation who are more mature in their faith will at this point have the opportunity to introduce inquirers who are not members of your congregation to Jesus Christ. The small groups are the heart of this program.

Including these seven key elements of the *Beginnings* experience ensures that the participants' journey together will be transforming for all of them.

INTRODUCING *BEGINNINGS*

When you first introduce *Beginnings* to your congregation, we suggest that you begin with a small group of people who will serve as the sponsors and leaders of the program over a longer period of time. This group might be the evangelism committee or the church council or a particular Sunday school class or simply a group of interested members.

A good way to begin is to view the first video/DVD presentation and discuss the questions in *Beginnings: Participant's Guide*. This will help the members of the leadership team understand the program and help them interpret it to potential participants.

Because congregations of any size can use *Beginnings*, the program will naturally vary in many ways. The program may range from eight-to-twelve persons meeting in a private apartment, home, or church parlor to hundreds of people who meet in a large-membership congregation's fellowship hall. A group smaller than eight may simply be too small to encourage good discussion, but there is almost no upper limit to the number of participants in the program (allowing, of course, for a sufficient number of small groups). The organizing principles in this chapter apply to groups of any size.

There are two ways to begin this program. One way is to begin with a group of seasoned congregation members who participate with the intention of becoming small-group leaders and hosts for future groups that would include unchurched or new-to-the-church participants. This way of starting the program gives you an opportunity to become familiar with *Beginnings* before you invite outside guests to take part.

The second way is to begin with a group of seasoned members and unchurched or new-to-the-church participants. If you begin this way, you will want to do careful preparation with the other members of the leadership team.

After your congregation has used *Beginnings* several times and has become familiar with the program, consider the advantages of having at least two programs a year, and maybe even as many as four. By presenting the program multiple times, participants in a previous program are quickly enabled to invite their friends to the next one. The best times to conduct the program are during the fall (September to November), the winter (January to March), or the spring (April to May).

Another time of year that works is during the summer (June to August). It is best not to interrupt the program with a major holiday season such as Christmas or Easter.

A NINE-WEEK OR TWELVE-WEEK MODEL?

Another key decision you must make is whether to run the twelve sessions of *Beginnings* over nine weeks or over twelve weeks. The nine-week model includes a Day Apart retreat during which you complete three sessions on a Saturday or Sunday. The twelve-week model simply offers one session each week. There are advantages and disadvantages to both models.

The key advantage to the nine-week model is that the program can be completed in a two-month period and avoids the possibility of having to interrupt the program for a major holiday. The Day Apart retreat is also an ideal way to conduct Sessions 7, 8, and 9, the heart of the program, in a place where serious conversation can occur without interruption. Participants will bond at a much higher level during such a day. The major disadvantage is that many people simply may not be able to schedule a one-day retreat, thus diminishing the program. If some of your participants cannot attend the Day Apart retreat, it is better not to use this model.

The main advantage of the twelve-week model is that you create a weekly rhythm that you maintain and do not vary. The commitment level required may appear to be a little lower, and thus the program may seem to be more accessible to some participants. The major disadvantage is that the program will take almost three months, and it may be more difficult to avoid a major holiday. Another disadvantage is that the community building may occur at a lower level. There is no right decision about which model to follow; either the nine-week or the twelve-week model may serve your congregation well. Simply decide which model is more appropriate to your community and the participants you wish to involve.

SCHEDULE

Set the dates for each weekly session (and the Day Apart retreat in the nine-week model) as far ahead of time as possible. Publish and distribute the schedule for the program throughout your publicity period; on the first day of the program, give a copy to every participant (see page 60).

Below are sample schedules (Typically you would not include the two training sessions in your publicity; they are included here for your information.). Please note that all of the sample forms throughout this chapter are also found in Chapter 9.

Nine-Week Model

Two weeks out	Training Session 1: Introduction to *Beginnings*
One week out	Training Session 2: Preparing for *Beginnings*
Week 1	Session 1: So, Is This All There Is? Introduction
Week 2	Session 2: Who Is Jesus, and Why Should I Care? Jesus Christ
Week 3	Session 3: Why Am I Not Where I Want to Be? Sin and the Cross
Week 4	Session 4: What Happens When I Die? Death and the Resurrection
Week 5	Session 5: Can I Trust God? Providence and Suffering
Week 6	Session 6: How Does God Speak to Me? The Bible

Day Apart (Sessions 7, 8, and 9 in one day)
Day Apart Schedule

Session 7:	If I Don't Feel Lost, Why Do I Need to Be Found? Salvation and Conversion
Session 8:	Can I Start Again? Forgiveness and Wholeness
Session 9:	How Do I Speak to God? Prayer
Week 7	Session 10: How Can I Make a Life and Not Just a Living? The Good Life
Week 8	Session 11: Why Should I Join Any Group That Will Have Me as a Member? Church
Week 9	Session 12: Love Feast! Remembering, Sharing, and Continuing the Journey

Twelve-Week Model

Two weeks out	Training Session 1: Introduction to *Beginnings*
One week out	Training Session 2: Preparing for *Beginnings*
Week 1	Session 1: So, Is This All There Is? Introduction
Week 2	Session 2: Who Is Jesus, and Why Should I Care? Jesus Christ
Week 3	Session 3: Why Am I Not Where I Want to Be? Sin and the Cross
Week 4	Session 4: What Happens When I Die? Death and the Resurrection
Week 5	Session 5: Can I Trust God? Providence and Suffering
Week 6	Session 6: How Does God Speak to Me? The Bible
Week 7	Session 7: If I Don't Feel Lost, Why Do I Need to Be Found? Salvation and Conversion
Week 8	Session 8: Can I Start Again? Forgiveness and Wholeness
Week 9	Session 9: How Do I Speak to God? Prayer
Week 10	Session 10: How Can I Make a Life and Not Just a Living? The Good Life
Week 11	Session 11: Why Should I Join Any Group That Will Have Me as a Member? Church Membership
Week 12	Session 12: Love Feast! Remembering, Sharing, and Continuing the Journey

In this book and in *Beginnings: Small-Group Leader's Guide*, we have included subheads for each of the twelve sessions. These subheads identify the major theological issues discussed in each session. These subheading, however, are for your planning only. These labels are not included in the sample forms, in *Beginnings: Participant's Guide*, or in *Beginnings: Along the Way: A Participant's Companion.*

ENVIRONMENT

Creating a hospitable setting for *Beginnings* is crucial as you plan for the sessions. Because *Beginnings* is a congregational program, most sessions may take place in your congregation's facilities. One way of creating a hospitable environment is by ensuring that your setting is accessible to persons who are physically challenged. Provide access for persons who are in wheelchairs and a good sound system for persons who are hard-of-hearing or when your group gets so large that participants have trouble hearing.

You can create a welcoming setting in other ways as well. Have directional signs to the location of the meal, restrooms, nursery/childcare, and the small-group meeting areas. Do not assume that everyone knows where everything is. Put a "Welcome" sign over the primary, outside entrance door. Set up a registration table; and put out nametags, a sign-up sheet for persons who did not register, and a place for congregational hosts to pay for the meal. As people gather, provide a place for them to leave coats and umbrellas and, if appropriate, a secure location for briefcases and handbags. In the dining area, provide centerpieces or table decorations; set the room temperature appropriately; and arrange tables and chairs so that participants can eat together in their small discussion groups. Set up a podium with a chalkboard, whiteboard, or flip chart, and write your housekeeping announcements on it. If you are meeting in a larger room, make sure that there is good lighting in the front presentation area. Because so much depends on hearing clearly, use a public address system if you expect more than a few dozen people. Finally, have everything set up before the first participants arrive; last minute set-up indicates lack of preparation and creates anxiety.

Serve the meal in your fellowship hall, a large classroom, or parlor. This same space may also be used for the singing, as well as the video/DVD presentation; or the participants may move to a nearby space so that your meal cleanup can take place without disturbing them. Because *Beginnings* is more of a teaching program than a worship program, it suggests more of an educational setting than a worship environment. The sanctuary, therefore, is generally not a good place for the presentation unless your sanctuary also serves as your fellowship area. The best environment for the video/DVD presenta-tion is one in which people are able to sit comfortably in semicircles or around tables so they can make notes in their copy of *Beginnings: Participant's Guide.*

Plan for sufficient small-group meeting tables, areas, or rooms. When you have multiple small groups, each group must have some private space where group members can sit in a circle or around a table, see one another clearly, and discuss freely and energetically without disturbing other groups. If your small groups are crowded together, the noise will seriously limit free discussion. Each small group should stay together and be able to use the same space throughout the program. Also be very careful about the relationship of the small-group space to the large gathering space. If persons are expected to move down a hall, up a flight of stairs, down another hall, and then make a left turn, many people may choose to head out the back door instead of to their small group. Every time people move from one space to another, some persons may disappear. If at all possible, keep people in or as close as possible to your gathering place.

Because childcare is crucial for young couples and single parents, provide adequate space and equipment for safe and secure care of children. Because children need security and consistency, try to maintain the same childcare staff throughout the program. Children need stability and a friendly face, not a new volunteer each week. If your congregation has regular childcare volunteers or staff who work on Sunday mornings, try to use these same people for childcare during *Beginnings.* Parents of small children will be more likely to return to your church on Sunday mornings if they know who the childcare providers are. In addition, because of increased concern about child safety, conduct a background check on your childcare providers and describe to parents how your congregation is committed to providing a safe environment for children. If the children are happy and safe, the parents will be happy and assured.

An alternative location for *Beginnings* is a setting very different from your congregation's facilities: a community center, a local cafeteria or restaurant, an athletic club or YMCA/YWCA, or an apartment complex clubhouse. Such a setting provides a safe haven for persons without a religious background, attracting a very different type of participant. As you plan your yearly calendar, seriously consider finding an alternative location for at least one of your programs each year. Doing so will make it easier for seekers and cultural Christians to discover your congregation.

A private home is another fine location for *Beginnings*. In this setting (usually for only four-to-six couples or eight-to-twelve persons total), the host family usually provides the meal. Then everyone gathers in a family room, den, or porch. In a program conducted in a private home, the host family may or may not be responsible for leading the small-group discussion. The preparation of meals may also be rotated among the members of the leadership team. After a few sessions, you may discover that there are a number of families who wish to host a session in their home.

Whatever setting you use, be sure there is room for a meal; a TV and VCR/DVD player; and enough chairs for people to sit in circles, see one another clearly, and hear one another well.

ADVERTISE

As you begin to make decisions about the program, prepare an attractive advertising brochure, promotional flyer, bulletin board, and signs with all the crucial details: date, place, time, cost, and phone number or website for information. (A *Beginnings* promotional package is also available from Cokesbury.) Use the *Beginnings* logo throughout your advertising. In addition, produce a one-page letter, which provides all the dates; and include a registration card (See Chapter 9. Reproducible Forms.). Set up a separate site on your congregational website (if you have one) to explain the program and facilitate on-line registration. Do not require registration, however, as walk-in participants should be expected and welcomed. Remember Jesus' parable of the king who gave a banquet; only those who were forgotten at first actually attended the feast. Throw your net wide!

Sample registration information (see page 58; again, all of the sample forms throughout this chapter are also found in Chapter 9. Reproducible Forms) is provided below:

Name:_____

Address:_____

Phone:_____

E-mail:_____

Childcare: Yes   No   Ages/Names of children:

Special Diet Requirements:

The following **optional** information will help us determine the right discussion group for you:

Age:_____

Gender:_____

Profession:_____

Marital Status:_____

Will you attend with a spouse or friend?   Yes   No

The best way to recruit participants is to involve your church members; a personal invitation is far superior to any written communication! Once members of your congregation have experienced the program, they will invite their friends. *Beginnings* helps you create a congregational culture in which members of your faith community feel comfortable inviting their friends, family, coworkers, and neighbors to participate in the program. Many Christians want to share their faith, but they simply do not know how; or they believe they do not have enough information. To assist your church members, advertise *Beginnings* for a month prior to the first session in your Sunday bulletin, website, and church newsletter. Set up a *Beginnings* bulletin board. Send e-mails to all congregation members, and ask them to forward the invitation to a friend. Give out brochures with the Sunday announcement bulletin. During the announcements in worship, explain *Beginnings*. Ask someone who has completed the program to speak for three minutes and give specific and concrete examples of her or his experience.

Special invitations may also be sent to your congregational members who have a gift for hospitality, persons with the gift of evangelism, parents wanting to have their children baptized, and adult baptism and baptismal reaffirmation candidates. Engaged couples who plan to have their wedding ceremony in your church building may also be invited to participate as part of their preparation for marriage. Some engaged couples may discover that *Beginnings* transforms not only their relationship with God but also their relationship with each other as they begin their married life. Finally, advertise the program during your special services that attract potential participants: children's musical performances, church preschool or daycare programs, vacation Bible school events, Sunday School Promotion Sunday, Rally Sunday, Scout Sunday, and worship services at Christmas and Easter.

In addition, on a Sunday prior to the start of the program, your worship leaders may wish to concentrate the worship service on a topic that would be of most interest to potential participants, such as, "Is Christianity Relevant?" On these Sundays, encourage members of your congregation to bring their friends, family members, neighbors, and coworkers who would not normally attend worship. At the end of the sermon, your pastor could suggest that women and men who would like to investigate Christianity further consider attending *Beginnings*. While potential participants may be asked to identify themselves and register for the program, understand that many persons may wish to remain anonymous until your program begins. Simply invite everyone to come to an introductory session or to the first session of *Beginnings*.

Finally, at the program's closing Love Feast, advertise the next time *Beginnings* will be held. See the description of the Love Feast on pages 105–107 for more details.

SAMPLE INVITATION

Beginnings: An Introduction to Christian Faith
We invite you to join a new *Beginnings* program.
September 10th–November 5th
Nine weeks on Wednesday evenings at Central United Methodist Church.
5:30 PM to 7:30 PM
Each session includes a meal, a presentation about basic Christian beliefs, and small discussion groups. Special Day Apart retreat on October 18th. Ideal for anyone who wants to learn more about the Christian faith. Wonderful opportunity to meet new people and make new friends.
Free childcare.
The meal and program are offered without cost to guests.
For more information, call xxx-xxx-xxxx or see www.xxxx.

ATTENDANCE

After the first session of your program, be prepared for the fact that fewer people may attend the following week. *Beginnings* is not for everyone. Up to fifty percent of all first-session participants may drop away by the end of the second or third week. Some people stop coming for good reasons: The time of day or the day of the week is just not going to work for them, or their lives are too complex. Other people analyze their schedules and realize they cannot commit to the entire program. When participants are irregular in their attendance, their occasional presence will create some anxiety and disruption. Suggest to everyone that while attendance is not mandatory and attendance sheets are not kept, no one should miss more than two sessions. If a participant misses more than two sessions, it is best for the person to stop and join the program the next time it is offered. Some people stop coming because of your leaders, the setting, or the presentations. These persons simply do not believe that the people or the community or the material is right for them. Other people may drop out for the reasons Jesus described in his parable of the sower (Matthew 13:1-8, 18-23): Some ground is too rocky, other ground is too thin, and still other ground is too covered with weeds. But do not despair; many of these persons may come back to attend the next time you offer the program, or a year later.

NAMETAGS

An individual's most personal possession is his or her name. Provide a nametag for each participant. Have the person's name on it and her or his small-group number or location. Make sure that children also have their own nametag for the sake of your childcare providers. A plastic nametag on a string or elastic thread may be the most economical in the long run. Since names are so important, be especially careful to spell everyone's name correctly. At the registration table, place the nametags in alphabetical order; and ask your hosts to help distribute the nametags. Give a different colored nametag to your *Beginnings* leadership team members, or print their names in a different color. This method allows participants who are not part of your congregation to know who these leaders are if they need to ask questions. Especially at the first session, have some blank nametags available for unexpected guests. Prepare a nametag the next week for these walk-in participants. Everyone, especially your leaders and congregation members, should continue wearing their nametags throughout the program; and hosts should concentrate on saying each person's name as often as possible.

RESOURCES

Provide the following for each participant:

Beginnings: Participant's Guide, the participant workbook

The Holy Bible, in a modern translation (NRSV or NIV)

A pen or pencil

Beginnings: Along the Way: A Participant's Companion

CONTACT SHEETS

At the first session, give each small-group leader a blank contact sheet (see page 61) to fill in the name of each participant and contact information: name, phone, e-mail. Help everyone understand that this contact information is being collected only for use in special circumstances, such as the need to cancel a session or to alert persons about a problem. You should not use the contact sheets to recruit people to congregational activities or to pursue people if they decide not to continue the program. The director should collect the contact sheets at the end of the first session, make a copy, and return the original to the small-group leader as soon as possible. The director should keep a copy of all the sheets, which will be used in a final evaluation. Do not give each participant or anyone else a copy of the contact sheet. If participants want to exchange addresses and telephone numbers, they can do so individually. If anyone contacts either the director or the small-group leader for this information, do not give it out under any circumstances. Respect and honor the privacy of the participants.

SAMPLE CONTACT SHEET

The following information will not be shared with members of the group or used to contact you except under special circumstances, such as the need to cancel a session or to alert persons about a problem.

Small Group:_____
Name:_____
Phone Number:_____
E-mail:_____

CHILDCARE

Many participants will be parents with younger children. Parents who are concerned about their child's religious development often begin to ask their own spiritual questions. Provide childcare at every session, including the training sessions (for your leadership team members) and the Day Apart retreat. Begin childcare fifteen minutes before the start of each session, and let parents know that childcare will continue fifteen minutes after the closing so that parents who wish to talk a little more will not be rushed. Because many couples and single parents live far from family and friends, arranging their own childcare for all the sessions can be quite difficult and expensive. If your congregation cares about the children, the parents will be sure that your congregation will also care about them. Make nametags for the children (These may need to go on the backs of the younger children.). Make sure that your childcare providers are trained and in an emergency know exactly where the parents will be in your facilities. Your congregation should also have in place policies—such as background checks and a minimum of two adults with the children at all times—that ensure the safe care of children. Share these policies with parents, who are becoming increasingly reluctant to leave a child with a congregational worker. Finally, the same persons should serve as childcare providers throughout the program; children do not want to meet a new babysitter and stranger every week. Pay the childcare providers out of the church budget, or charge a nominal fee.

QUESTIONNAIRES

Evaluations of the program by the participants will give you a way to monitor the quality of the program and help you constantly improve. We recommend that each participant receive a questionnaire during Session 11 (see page 64). This survey provides your leadership team with assistance in evaluating the program and its leaders and help in planning the next program.

Also, during Session 11, give the small-group leaders their own questionnaire about their experience of the program (see page 65). Your leaders will also be asked to complete a second leader questionnaire. This second questionnaire is based on the original contact sheets (see page 61), with the name of each group member. Ask your leaders about the members of their group. For example, one form asks your small-group leaders which of their initial group members completed the program and if a person did not complete the program, do they know why. Also, ask your small-group leaders to describe briefly how their group members are going to continue their spiritual journey. To prepare for the Love Feast, ask your small-group leaders which participants could give a good witness to God's work in their lives. Finally, ask which participants might be good *Beginnings* helpers during a future program. The program is only as good as your leaders, and the questionnaires will assist you in evaluating the work of each of your small-group leaders.

SAMPLE PARTICIPANT QUESTIONNAIRE
(Please turn in today or no later than next week.)

Name_____
Small Group_____

1. How did you learn about *Beginnings*?
2. Why did you decide to attend?
3. How did you benefit from *Beginnings*?
4. What did you enjoy most about *Beginnings?*
5. What did you find most difficult?
6. How could the program be improved?
7. Other comments:
8. Are you willing to assist in a future *Beginnings* program?

SAMPLE LEADER QUESTIONNAIRE
(Please turn in today or no later than next week.)

Name_____
Small Group_____
Position _____

1. How did you become a small-group leader?
2. How did you benefit from *Beginnings*?
3. What did you find most difficult?
4. How could the program be improved?
5. Other comments:

6. Are you willing to be a small-group leader in a future *Beginnings* program?

SAMPLE SMALL-GROUP LEADER EVALUATION OF PARTICIPANTS
(Please turn in next week.)

Describe your small-group members, including: level of participation, next steps in their spiritual journey, ability to offer a testimony at the Love Feast, and possibility of becoming a helper in the next program:

Name
 Completed course?   Y   N
If not, do you know why?
Able to offer witness at love feast?   Y   N
Possible helper in a future program?   Y   N
Other comments:

AFTER *BEGINNINGS*

Because small groups are the heart of this program, members of your small groups develop strong friendships and often want to remain together as small groups after the program ends. Celebrate this commitment to a small group, and help people build on these experiences. Some small groups may continue as a weekly Bible study group or as a new Sunday school class. Be aware, however, that not everyone in every group will want to continue meeting regularly with these particular people. In the larger scheme of things, participants who wish to continue the journey in your congregation need to be integrated into the life of your Christian community. There are many appropriate ways of incorporating persons into your congregation. People may be invited to join an existing Sunday school class, to come to worship, to participate in an ongoing Bible study, or to take part in another small-group activity.

For persons who want to know more and to grow in serious discipleship, other courses and programs are available, such as the DISCIPLE Bible Study, *Companions in Christ*, *Witness*, JESUS IN THE GOSPELS and CHRISTIAN BELIEVER. Each of these programs provides substantially more content and has very specific and high expectations of participants. In addition, there are a number of well-written introductions to Christianity which may be appropriate and helpful to all participants. Several of these include William Placher's *Jesus: The Savior*, an introduction to Jesus' life and teaching; Thomas Cahill's *Desire of the Everliving Hills*, a summary of the life of Jesus and his impact on Western culture; and William McDonald's *Gracious Voices*, a series of readings from major persons in church history for people beginning the spiritual journey. Leaders in your congregation may also have other recommendations. Remember, however, that many seekers, cultural Christians, and even new Christians take a long time to begin to participate in the life of any congregation. A lack of immediate response by participants does not mean the program has failed. Many of your guests will return in the months and years to come. The seeds have been sown; let them germinate at their own pace.

Keep in mind that when one *Beginnings* program ends, another begins. May God bless your continuing work as the ripple effects of this program continue.

5.
Leaders and Their Responsibilities

Jesus said to his disciples, "Follow me, and I will make you fish for people" (Matthew 4:19). Today, Jesus Christ still calls those of us who follow him to imitate him and reach out to other people. The success of *Beginnings: An Introduction to Christian Faith* does not depend upon this book or Rob's presentations or the free Bibles or the meals. Its success depends upon leaders like you who, in the power of God's Holy Spirit, guide each program in your congregation. While God is in ultimate control of this program, God does choose to work through gracious persons in your congregation. Like the spiritual companions that Dante Alighieri found in his journey toward heaven in the *Divine Comedy* or Gandalf the Wizard who led Frodo the Hobbit in his quest to return the ring, all followers of Jesus Christ need people like you who will guide them along the path God intends. When God invites persons in your congregation to reach out to their friends, neighbors, family members, coworkers, and other inquirers, God also calls leaders and gives these leaders the skills necessary to help people in their journey toward Jesus Christ. Throughout this chapter, we will address directly the various key leadership team members.

TO THE LEADERSHIP TEAM

The leadership team consists of the servant guides who enable this program. You are the companions for inquirers on the way; you are the midwives who make new birth in Christ possible in your congregation. Within this program, you and each of the other guides may have only one task; or you may have multiple assignments. The leadership team members are the hands, feet, ears, and mouths of the body of Christ, who make visible to all the participants Jesus Christ himself.

Your leadership team may be large or small, depending on the number of people who will participate in *Beginnings*; but you will need persons who will fill the following positions: pastor, director, small-group leader, music/worship leader, meal coordinator and preparers, treasurer, and helpers.

In programs with a smaller group of participants, not every task or assignment needs a different person; as few as two people can lead a program for eight other people. In some programs, the pastor may also be the director and a small-group leader. The meal coordinator and the music/worship leader may also be small-group helpers.

The goal is for you to have the right number of leadership team members, so that everyone has a significant role to play but no one is overwhelmed by the responsibilities.

QUALIFICATIONS AND REQUIREMENTS

God "equip[s] the saints for the work of ministry, for building up the body of Christ" (Ephesians 4:12). The most important task in starting *Beginnings* is forming a leadership team from your congregation. Leaders and helpers from your host congregation should consist of about one third of the total number of people in the program.

The members of your leadership team must be confident in their faith, gracious to guests, familiar with Scripture, comfortable with small groups, and attentive to the movement of the Holy Spirit in a group. Your leadership team members do not necessarily need to be longtime Christians, but they should be passionate about their care of other people and willing to share their faith. It is vital to choose the right people.

Throughout *Beginnings* you and all the members of the leadership team will work hard and must have a high level of commitment. If the members of your leadership team do not regularly attend the sessions, the participants will be unlikely to do so. Hosts must do the necessary preparation, attend regularly, talk with guests, and concentrate on the task.

When you identify and approach possible leadership team members, be clear about the commitment required, which is for two training sessions, twelve regular sessions, and follow-up after the program to welcome and possibly incorporate guests into your congregational community. Strongly encourage all your leadership team members to come to every session. If some leadership team members are unable to come to the training, ask them to review the relevant sections of this book or *Beginnings: Small-Group Leader's Guide*. Even if some members of your leadership team have helped with several programs or feel they are experts in small groups, they should still come to the two training sessions for every program.

Prayer is an essential part of this commitment. All your leadership team members need to pray regularly for every aspect of *Beginnings*: the worship, the video/DVD presentations, and the individual members of your leadership team. They must also commit themselves to pray for every participant in their small group.

Finally, be assured that your program will be ultimately successful, not because of the skills of your leadership team members, but because of God's grace. God alone inspires your leaders, the Holy Spirit empowers your team, and the destination is clearly God's kingdom. When the first disciples chose laypeople to become servant-leaders (deacons) in the new church in Jerusalem, the community chose persons like Stephen who were "full of the Spirit and of wisdom" (Acts 6:3). Stephen did not begin his work having all the skills he needed, but over time he became one of the most gifted followers of Jesus Christ. Saintly people, called by God and gifted with the Spirit, are present in your local congregation and empowered for sharing the feast.

TO THE PASTOR

As the pastor of your local congregation, the shepherd of the people of God, you are the key to *Beginnings*. As the spiritual guide of your congregation, you must demonstrate strong, visible, and vocal support if *Beginnings* is to succeed. You may serve as the director, the song leader, or simply the first greeter throughout the sessions. Especially in the first years your congregation hosts *Beginnings,* you must demonstrate enthusiastic support for this program in your congregation. The first time or few times your congregation hosts *Beginnings*, you will want to consider being the director.

TO THE DIRECTOR

Since you are the director, this manual should be your constant companion. The key gifts required of you are organization; leadership; and the ability to create a team atmosphere in which the eyes, hands, feet, mouths, and hearts all work together.

As director you have a number of specific responsibilities. You may carry them out yourself, or you may delegate them to other members of the leadership team.

Select, train, guide, and encourage all your leadership team members.

Plan the schedule, choose the setting, and perform other preliminary tasks.

Design and promote the program.

Start each session on time.

State the focus of each session.

Set the tone for each gathering.

Involve everyone.

Have fun, and grow spiritually.

Close the sessions on time.

Write thank you notes to your leadership team members at the end of the program.

While you are ultimately responsible for every aspect of the program, you may also assign other members of the leadership team the following specific responsibilities:

Design promotional material.

Prepare the setting/environment/space for each session.

Register hosts and guests, providing nametags to everyone.

Put up directional signs, including a sign for each small group.

Clean up at the end of each session.

If each and every one of your congregational hosts has one or two specific tasks, they will all claim ownership of the whole program; and the work will be manageable for everyone as a result.

TO THE SMALL-GROUP LEADERS

Your work is most important; you personally guide each participant into a relationship with Jesus Christ. Like Jesus' disciples, you are fishing for people. Please read carefully the material in the next chapter, Small Groups, for a detailed discussion of your responsibilities.

TO THE MUSIC/WORSHIP LEADER

Music touches people's emotions, proclaims the faith, and points women and men toward God. During *Beginnings,* you may guide a brief time of singing at the start of each weekly session; or you may have singing only at the Love Feast. Not every program needs to have singing and music each week. It will depend on your congregation's practice and the size of your group. However you involve music in this program, your goal is to build community and to give all participants songs for the road.

If you decide to have weekly singing or a musical presentation, you need a song leader with an easy-to-follow voice. These few minutes may be a time for solos and also for some enjoyable singing with everyone joining in, such as singing "Happy Birthday" to a participant. You may use a keyboard (not a pipe organ), a guitar, or simply your own voice without accompaniment. Your style should be graciously hospitable and confident. Use just a few words of introduction that lead into the singing. In this leadership role, it is your responsibility to offer a musical experience for all the participants that helps them bond with one another.

We suggest that you avoid using hymnals and sanctuary songbooks for the singing. Such books may have an institutional feel and may look overwhelming. Instead, if possible, use slides, transparencies, and computer-generated projection slides to provide words on a screen. If you do choose to copy music, be sure that you follow copyright laws by securing permission or subscribing to groups such as Christian Copyright Licensing, Incorporated.

Some of your participants may feel uncomfortable singing in public. If they choose not to sing, that is all

right. You can encourage singing by using familiar songs, however. If you choose to have weekly singing, start at the first session with only about five minutes of singing by you or a song leader alone. Then progress to involving the participants. Keep the period of music brief, and move from more secular music during the first sessions to more Christian music by the end of the program. One reasonable goal for you is to enable participants to experience the joy of singing with other people, so that when a participant who is not a member of your congregation shows up at worship, the experience of singing will feel natural to her or him.

Finally, as the music/worship leader you are also responsible for any other musicians, for any musical instruments, for overhead transparencies or slides or computer-generated video projection, and for set up and monitoring of all the sound equipment, as well as for the Love Feast music at the end of the program.

TO THE MUSIC/MEAL COORDINATOR

Just as Jesus ate meals with sinners, at Zacchaeus's home in Jericho, beside the Sea of Galilee with thousands, in Mary and Martha's Bethpage residence, and in an upper room with his disciples, so Christians continue to reach out to everyone over food and drink. As the meal coordinator you are responsible for the food and all the related activities. Your responsibilities include ordering food and beverages, setting up tables and chairs for the meal, as well as cleaning up the kitchen and dining area after the meal. Also, you ensure there are enough plates, cups, silverware, tea, coffee, and condiments for meals and breaks. Feel free to recruit assistants, or use some of the small-group helpers to assist in the preparation and serving of the meals.

Maintaining a tight schedule is a key to the success of the program, and the meal and breaks will either cause delays or guarantee that the schedule is kept. You, therefore, must see to it that the meals and breaks are served on time and in a quick manner (no long lines), that dishes are returned or taken up promptly, and that the cleanup (especially the activity and noise) not interfere with the opening welcome by your director or with the discussion within small groups.

When the leadership team is few in numbers, various team members may wish to assist with the cooking by choosing various weeks to do so. Or the cooking may be assigned to the small groups on a rotating basis. But be careful; too many cooks can spoil the soup and begin a session on a sour note. Your congregation may also employ a caterer or church-meal coordinator as the meal coordinator.

MEALS AND BREAKS

Food is an important part of *Beginnings*. All of your participants can relax, calm down, and prepare for serious dialogue after a hectic day while visiting over a meal or at a noon-time break. Keep your standards for the food as high as possible.

The following options are suggestions for food during *Beginnings*; additional suggestions are found in Chapter 10. Meals. In general, appropriate foods might include simple pasta dishes, casseroles, waffles/pancakes, Brunswick stew, pizza, hamburgers, hot dogs, salads, special dishes that will appeal to your participants, or dishes distinctive to your congregation's region or culture. Your congregation may even share its own distinctive meals, such as a favorite casserole or foods out of your congregational cookbook. Use the following suggestions, and then be creative:

1. Vegetarian Meals: Be sure that you always offer a vegetarian alternative when a meat dish is served. As meal coordinator you may wish to ask at the first session how many participants would like vegetarian options; then prepare accordingly. Variety is less important than sensitivity to the particular needs of vegetarians. Hospitality is the key.

2. Drinks: Provide good coffees and teas, both hot and cold, both caffeinated and decaffeinated. In addition, offer a variety of colas, clear sodas, powdered mixes, bottled water, and ice. After the first few sessions, it will become apparent what the drinks of choice will be. To encourage conversation, allow participants to take a drink with them to the video/DVD presentation and to their group discussion. Making drinks available at the end of the session will encourage people to stay for a few more minutes of conversation. Again, hospitality is the key.

3. Desserts: Provide homemade and high quality cookies, brownies, ice cream sandwiches, or other ice cream novelties. Allow persons to eat their dessert during the presentation. Having additional desserts at the end of the session will encourage participants to stay for further dialogue. You may wish to invite your congregation to prepare desserts as a way of involving additional members of your congregation in this program.

4. Breaks for programs that do not include a full meal (for example, mid-morning programs): Provide a wide variety of drinks, such as multiple kinds of teas and cold drinks, as well as some simple salty and sweet finger foods. Peanuts and small chocolate candies may be sufficient. When breaks alone are the occasion for food, invest a little more money for attractive cups, plates, and napkins.

TO THE TREASURER

You will need to manage the financial details of the program. This may include purchasing copies of materials, advancing money for meals, collecting food money from your congregational members who attend, paying childcare workers, and keeping an accurate accounting of all money received and spent. You may also manage finances for a book table that provides related materials for participants.

We suggest that it is best not to charge guest participants who are not members of your host congregation. Your congregation may want to budget for *Beginnings* as part of its outreach or evangelism ministry. The number one reason people say they stay away from congregations is that many people outside the church believe that the church is after their money. You and your congregation, therefore, must create an environment in which it is clear that everyone cares more about the participants and less about the cost of the program.

There are additional ways to cover the cost of the program. For example, a simple basket may be placed at the end of the serving line for donations from everyone who attends; some people simply do not want to feel indebted to others for a meal. Or participants who are members of your congregation may be asked to contribute to the cost of their meal plus that of one guest. Again, what is important to remember is that people are more important than money. Try to arrange things so that no one is made to feel uncomfortable.

Budget items might include:

Beginnings Getting Started Kit (includes *Beginnings: Director's Manual; Beginnings: Video Resources; Beginnings: Small-Group Leader's Guide; Beginnings: Participant's Guide; Beginnings: Along the Way: A Participant's Companion;* and promotional materials)
Additional *Beginnings* resources
Advertising (brochures, posters, yard signs, postage)
Bibles
Supplies (pens, pencils, and nametags)
Meals
Day Apart expenses
Love Feast expenses
Childcare expenses

TO THE TEAM COORDINATOR AND SUPPORT TEAM
(For Programs With Over Forty Participants)

When there are a large number of participants, your leadership team members need additional helpers. As team coordinator you handle for the director some of the logistical details for a large program so that your director may concentrate on participants and program content. You need to be organized, comfortable with details, and possess a humble spirit that willingly takes on tasks to free up your director and other leadership team members for ministry. For example, you may assign the different tasks, such as registration, room set-up, cleanup at

the end of each session, and so forth. In a program with a large number of participants, you may also be in charge of a support group of willing volunteers. Finally, you may also provide for the pastoral needs of the other leadership team members, making sure that everyone receives the necessary spiritual support throughout the program.

Programs with a large number of participants require, in addition to a team coordinator, a support team of helpers: women and men who are willing to serve in any capacity. These support people from your congregation perform practical tasks such as putting up signs, cooking, cleaning up the kitchen, moving tables and chairs, and cleaning up the space at the end of the evening. These volunteers typically will not take part in the small groups because they are usually fully occupied with the practical tasks. Their love and service are in themselves a powerful witness to the love of Christ to those persons who are in the program. The team coordinator is ultimately responsible for these persons.

SUMMARY

Remember, the success of *Beginnings* depends on your leadership team members who guide each program in your congregation. When these persons reach out to their friends, neighbors, family members, coworkers, and other inquirers, God gives these leaders the skills necessary to share the Lord's banquet graciously with everyone.

6.
Weekly Sessions

You may hold a session of *Beginnings* in the morning, at midday, or in the evening. The most popular times may be in the evening, but daytime courses also have strengths that you should not overlook.

EVENING COURSES

The time for your evening sessions may vary dramatically, depending on the location and the work schedules of your participants. An evening session may begin as early as 4:30 PM or start as late as 7:30 PM.

One possible evening schedule for *Beginnings* follows this outline:

5:00 PM	Leader Orientation and Prayer by Director
5:20 PM	Leader Orientation Ends Participants Begin to Arrive and Are Greeted
5:30 PM	Supper Provided by Meal Coordinator
6:15 PM	Welcome by Director
6:20 PM	Singing by Worship Leader (optional)
6:25 PM	Video/DVD Presentation
6:45 PM	Small-Group Discussion
7:25 PM	Closing and Prayer
7:30 PM	Adjournment

At 5:00 PM, gather all your leadership team members for organization and prayer. During this time, the director guides a brief discussion of the theme of the session and any necessary housekeeping details. Every leadership team member should assist by mentioning other details that must be attended to if the session is to go well. This preparation time ends with prayer led by the director or a person named by her or him. End the orientation meeting at least ten minutes prior to supper so that the leadership team members may go out and welcome the gathering participants.

At 5:30 PM, the meal coordinator and assistants serve the meal. Eating together is an essential part of the program. During the meal, there should be no agenda other than encouraging people to visit with one another in a relaxed way. Typically, the members of each small group sit together; your leaders and helpers act as hosts and facilitate the conversations. The goal of the meal is to make friends. About ten minutes before the opening Welcome, the director reminds everyone about the schedule so that plates may be returned, drinks refilled, last desserts picked up, and restroom breaks taken before the Welcome.

At 6:15 PM, the director welcomes everyone briefly. A relaxing welcome from the director breaks down barriers and helps people relax. Humor is appropriate and helps participants experience the joy of Christian life. After a lighthearted word of welcome, talk about housekeeping details such as the Day Apart retreat, the Love Feast, questionnaires, or special events in your congregation that participants might appreciate attending. But remember, this is not a time for in-house congregational announcements or business.

At 6:20 PM, the music/worship leader may choose to have a brief time of music. While Paul suggested to us that we "sing psalms and hymns and spiritual songs among [ourselves], singing and making melody to the Lord in [your] hearts" (Ephesians 5:19), this is not a time primarily to teach Christian music. This brief time of music may be as simple as singing "Happy Birthday" or "Happy Anniversary" to the appropriate people or singing a simple Christian or popular chorus. As *Beginnings* continues, the music may move towards more overtly Christian choruses and songs. The length of time spent in singing may increase from about five minutes at the first session to no more than fifteen minutes by the end of the program. Some participants may not be ready to participate in the singing, and no one should be pressured to sing. Some groups, especially those that are small and meet in homes, may do without any singing. Singing, however, creates community in ways that conversation does not. Singing also helps inquirers take the first few steps from *Beginnings* to the sanctuary, where the worship of God is central.

At 6:25 PM, the director starts the video/DVD presentation featuring Rob Weber. The video/DVD presents the core biblical narrative and begins to engage key questions. *Beginnings: Participant's Guide* contains the biblical text for the session, a summary of the presentation, and some leading questions. There is also "white space" that encourages people to jot down some notes. Pens and pencils should be available.

At 6:45 PM, the director invites everyone to break into assigned small groups. The small-group leaders guide the discussion in the small groups. (See Chapter 7 in *Beginnings: Small- Group Leader's Guide* for more information.) Encourage people to move quickly to their meeting places. As you plan, be very careful about the relationship of the small-group space to the large gathering space. Every time people move from one space to another, persons may disappear. If at all possible, keep persons in or as close as possible to your gathering area.

At 7:25 PM, the small-group leaders close the conversations in their small groups and end with prayer. People are dismissed from their small groups without returning to the larger group.

At 7:30 PM, the session is over; participants may leave. While some persons will wish to remain and talk together, no one should be forced to stay beyond the announced ending time. All the members of the leadership team should remain until all the participants have left and then gather for a few moments to make plans for the next session.

DAYTIME PROGRAMS

Daytime programs may be held on a weekday or Saturday morning or afternoon. Such a program is for persons who may find it easier to attend sessions during the day rather than in the evening. There are obvious categories of participants who fit this profile: people with young children, persons who are self-employed or unemployed, people who work afternoons and evenings, and individuals who would prefer not to go out at night. A program held during the daytime can be just as successful as one conducted in the evening.

Daytime groups may work best meeting in a home; but they also work very well in a congregational fellowship hall, church parlor, or apartment complex clubhouse—provided there is room for childcare. Childcare for younger children is absolutely essential for a daytime program. If your congregation has a preschool, parent's morning out program, or daycare center, one ideal time for *Beginnings* would be a weekday morning. When parents drop off their children, the parents may then move down the hall to take part in *Beginnings*.

The biggest danger to avoid when conducting a daytime program is to let just one or two people lead and host the entire program. Because daytime programs tend to be smaller, you or someone else may even be tempted to believe that you can do it all by yourself. The difficulty with only one or a few people leading the program is that these persons will end up concentrating on the organizational details rather than on the participants. Remember that it is more important to talk with the participants than to run down the hall to fill up the coffee pot. Even in a daytime program, try to find enough congregational hosts to be about one third of the persons taking part in it.

Another difficulty with a daytime program that is smaller in participation is that singing may be more difficult. While even small groups can sing, persons are more self-conscious of their voices and musical ability in a small group. An advantage, however, that the absence of music may present is that you may add additional time for sharing and discussion.

One possible morning schedule for *Beginnings* follows this outline:

9:30 AM	Leader Orientation and Prayer
9:45 AM	Leader Orientation Ends
9:45 AM	Participants Begin to Arrive
10:00 AM	Refreshments
10:15 AM	Welcome by Director

10:20 AM	Singing (optional)
10:25 AM	Video/DVD Presentation
10:45 AM	Refreshment Break
10:55 AM	Small-Group Discussion
11:45 AM	Closing and Prayer
11:50 AM	Adjournment

Notice that this schedule provides for no meal, but there is more time for drinks and refreshments along with light conversation. (See page 38 for more details about drinks and food for morning programs.) Use the gathering and two refreshment break times for participants to meet one another and establish friendships rather than to discuss the content of the presentation. This schedule also allows more time for small-group discussion, which may facilitate deeper conversation.

One possible midday schedule for *Beginnings* follows this outline:

11:30 AM	Leader Orientation and Prayer
11:45 AM	Leader Orientation Ends
11:45 AM	Participants Begin to Arrive
12:00 noon	Lunch by Meal Coordinator
12:25 PM	Welcome by Director
12:30 PM	Singing Led by Music/Worship Leader (optional)
12:35 PM	Video/DVD Presentation
12:55 PM	Small-Group Discussion
1:35 PM	Closing and Prayer
1:40 PM	Adjournment

The midday program cuts down on your time for the meal and ends a little early compared to other programs. Be aware that some participants may have to leave a few minutes early to go to work or to pick up a child. In these situations, therefore, jump into the more serious questions more quickly; or simply plan to end before too many people have to leave.

Having a daytime program may mean you cannot have a Day Apart retreat as a one-day event. In that case you will need to have three additional daytime sessions. As a result, the program will require twelve weeks instead of nine. The first time a daytime program is scheduled, plan it for twelve weeks instead of nine. It is easier for you to decide after the program begins to have a one-day Day Apart retreat and cut out the last three sessions than to try to schedule three additional days at the end.

The Love Feast at the end of a daytime program, whether a morning or a midday program, may be a noon meal, although an evening meal may also suit your participants' schedules. Several weeks before the Love Feast, ascertain the best time for your closing celebration. This meal is an excellent opportunity for participants to bring their spouses and friends with them and gives everyone a wonderful opportunity to hear ordinary people talk about the gospel in a relaxed environment. Many spouses and friends of participants in a daytime program may eventually want to attend future sessions of *Beginnings*.

7.
Small Groups

Wade Clark Roof, in his book *A Generation of Seekers,* describes how many people in the baby-boomer generation are returning to religious communities for help in addressing three major issues in their lives: answering their children's religious questions, engaging in a personal spiritual quest, and finding an accepting community. In their search, while worship and large-group gatherings are important, even more critical are small groups for "sharing, caring, accepting, and belonging."[1] To meet these spiritual needs, Christian congregations are providing small groups, from Sunday school classes to book clubs to investment clubs to volleyball teams to twelve-step groups. The small-group community your congregation provides through *Beginnings* is almost as important as the theological content of the program. (Please note that much of the material in this chapter is included in the second chapter of *Beginnings: Small-Group Leader's Guide*, which is essential for each of your small-group leaders. It is included here so that directors can understand and support the work of small-group leaders.)

The small-group discussion, which follows the video/DVD presentation each week, brings all the participants in your group into a relationship with one another; with your congregation; and, most importantly, with Jesus Christ. Just as Jesus chose twelve ordinary people to be his first followers, so Jesus promised to be present whenever two or three persons are gathered together in his name (Matthew 18:20).

SIZE

Jesus chose twelve people to be his most intimate companions. Small groups should range in size from no less than six persons to no more than twelve (including all leaders and helpers). Eight-to-ten persons seems to be an ideal size. Approximately one-third of the members of each of your small groups should be leaders and helpers from your congregation.

SETTING

Like a teenager, every small group needs its own space. The director or team coordinator ensures that each group has enough chairs and that each group has a sign (either a number or the name of the small-group leader) to identify itself. Keep the space for each of your groups at or as close as possible to your main gathering place and dining area. Each group should sit in a circle or around a table. Everyone should be able to see the face of everyone else clearly and to hear plainly. Light, temperature, and ventilation need to be appropriate to the time of day and season of the year. Give each group enough space to encourage free, honest, and lively conversation without outside interruptions. The small groups should be able to use the same space each week.

Prior to your first meeting, the group helpers distribute Bibles and copies of *Beginnings: Participant's Guide* in their small-discussion-group rooms/areas. Have copies of a modern translation of the Bible (often provided by your congregation) for all participants to use during the sessions and to take home with them. We encourage you to offer these Bibles as gifts to the participants. At the first session, place the Bibles under one of the chairs or on a side table in each small-group meeting area. Doing this prevents seekers and cultural Christians from being intimidated by seeing Bibles everywhere. After the first session, it is helpful to have a few extra Bibles on hand for people who forget their copy.

PLACING PARTICIPANTS IN SMALL GROUPS

How you place participants in a small group is crucial; each participant should be able to look at the other people in the group and see someone who is similar to her or him. No one wants to be the odd person out. This is a task for the director, team coordinator, or possibly the whole leadership team working together. Organize your small groups just a day or two before the program starts. By waiting until the last days, you can compose the small groups from the whole group of leadership team members and participants; and everyone can have a preprinted or handwritten nametag.

Begin by selecting a team of hosts from your congregation to participate in each small group. Name one of your congregational hosts as the small-group leader and the others as helpers. The small-group leader and one helper should come to your opening organizational meeting every week.

Next, assign the participants to a small group. Even though you are using a registration form (see page 58), you may have little information about the participants who are not part of your congregation. During your two training sessions, the whole leadership team should review the list to assist in creating the right groups. For example, if a participant has a friend on your leadership team, put the two of them in the same group. Put married couples in the same group unless they ask not to be placed together. A goal for the first session is for all participants to know at least one person in their small group. By the end of the program everyone should know well everyone else in their small group.

If additional information is available about participants, arrange the small groups primarily by age; that is, keep persons with other people around their same age. In addition, groups may be formed around social background, marital status, age of children, and profession. Make your groups as compatible as possible. Keeping a balance between women and men in a group is also wise, but some groups may work best if the group is all men or all women. Do not put only one man or only one woman in a group.

Ultimately, remember that each participant is an individual. People need to be in a group of people where they will feel comfortable. Persons experience high stress when joining a new group in which most people are strangers. If persons are uncomfortable in their group, they probably will not come back. If you discover that someone wishes to move to a different group, make the change by the next session without making a major fuss.

Finally, because walk-ins may be expected, never fill up each small group prior to your first session; leave a couple of open slots to fill at the first session. It is better to have a few less people in each group than a few people too many.

CHOOSING SMALL-GROUP LEADERS

Choosing small-group leaders may be the director's single most important task. Jesus most often taught his disciples about the kingdom of God, not in formal teaching forums like the Sermon on the Mount, but during informal dialogues as they journeyed together. Discussion, not teaching, is the model of *Beginnings*. As persons hear the gospel through your leadership team members, helpers, and other participants, everyone grows spiritually. At each session, small groups discuss the video/DVD presentation and issues arising out of the presentation and respond to the basic questions that are addressed. This discussion period gives everyone the opportunity to respond to what they have heard, to share their experiences, and to ask questions. Asking questions is especially important if a small group is made up predominantly of persons who are not yet believers or part of your Christian community.

THE ROLE OF SMALL-GROUP LEADERS

As a small-group leader you guide all the participants toward Jesus Christ. In this task you are acting just like Jesus' first disciple, Simon Peter. In the Gospel of Mark, the first words of Jesus to Simon the fisherman were, "Follow me and I will make you fish for people" (Mark 1:17). Then, in John's Gospel, Jesus' last words to Simon the Rock were to "feed" and "tend" the people of God (John 21:15-19). You truly are the Peter-like companion on the journey for every participant in your small group.

Your goal as a small-group leader is to enable spiritual

growth along God's way by each group member. Your task is to encourage each person to understand and to be open to the grace of God in her or his own life. Even though the group members have heard the same content through the presentation, the basis for your group discussion is not "What did the presenter intend to say?" but "How does this biblical story and presentation connect to your life or illuminate your experiences?" The questions we provide for each session assist you with this work, but our experience has shown that people are eager to talk as soon as the presentation is over. The members of your small group simply need a wise guide to shape their conversation.

In light of this approach, you do not need to provide "correct" answers to questions. Instead, you need to provide an environment in which possible answers are explored and additional questions may be asked. In response to these presentations, a good discussion is not a debate about any particular person's ideas but a mutual sharing of experiences and opinions. Even though your group members will have heard the same presentation, your group discussions may move in unexpectedly different directions. Do your best to be open to the movement of the Holy Spirit and to be vigilant in discerning the difference between following the Spirit's lead and going off on a side road. Working in partnership with the Holy Spirit, who alone can bring about spiritual transformation, you may achieve marvelous things. Your success as a small-group leader will not be judged by what your group members "know" by the end of this program but by the way their lives are changed in the months and years to come.

In summary, your role as a small-group leader in *Beginnings* differs from that of a traditional teacher of a church school class or a small-group facilitator. You will read and study each week the material in *Beginnings: Small-Group Leader's Guide* and *Beginnings: Along the Way: A Participant's Companion*, watch and listen to the video/DVD presentations along with the participants in your small group, and facilitate your participants in sharing with the group. You may offer your own honest reflections, but your main goal is to help your group members listen carefully to one another and to the Holy Spirit. You are the one who leads your participants in a movement from the head to the heart to the hands and feet.

THE GIFTS OF SMALL-GROUP LEADERS

Leading small groups requires particular gifts and skills. As you guide your small-group members toward Jesus Christ, you need a variety of God-given gifts, including patience, care, support, encouragement, openness, silence, peace, and prayer. In addition, you must be fully prepared for each session, gently guide the conversation, avoid fixing problems, and watch the clock. When God enables you to exhibit these gifts and skills, all the participants can be confident about their guide and companion in the way toward Jesus Christ.

1. Patience is among the qualities that you need most as a discussion leader. Be patient, and let the Holy Spirit guide the process. While you may wish for rapid success, we encourage you to remember that the development of a relationship with Jesus Christ is a lifelong process. It may be difficult to identify any great leap on any particular day, but over time God is at work in the life of every person. Trust the work of the Holy Spirit as you meet with your small group.

2. Care for each person in your small group. Good shepherds watch carefully over each of their sheep. The aim of *Beginnings* is that every single person should be nurtured, which is why you have multiple congregational hosts in your small group. After the first session, assign one of your small-group hosts to take responsibility for two or three of the participants in your small group. Care for participants can be shown in a number of ways. For example, if one of your participants misses a session, it is your responsibility to check and be sure nothing is wrong. Be careful, however, not to be too aggressive in this shepherding. It is appropriate to telephone or e-mail participants if they miss a session and to express concern and offer appropriate support. If a participant was sick, send a get-well card and provide a summary of what happened during the session. If a participant did not have transportation, offer to arrange a ride. It is, however, inappropriate to call a participant and berate her or him for missing a session. If a participant wants to end the relationship or stop coming to the sessions, let him or her go with a prayer. This system of one-to-one care is one of the most crucial aspects of *Beginnings*.

3. Support spiritual growth. While spiritual maturity cannot develop overnight, you can assist your participants through the early stages of their walk of faith and later help integrate them into a congregational group once they have completed *Beginnings*. In general, you should tend to be more active earlier in the program, when people do not know one another well, and then back away as your group matures. Be attuned to the interests of your group members so that when they have completed *Beginnings*, you are prepared to guide them to other experiences within your congregation. The goal is to support participants in their ongoing Christian journey. Furthermore, if participants who are not members of your congregation start attending worship services in your church, arrange to meet and sit with them. Also encourage them to become involved in various congregational activities.

Part of encouraging spiritual maturity is to help participants avoid becoming attached to any leader other than Jesus Christ. Beware of any unhealthy dependence by any of the participants upon any leader. Instead, encourage your group members to grow in their relationships with a variety of people within the weekly gatherings and maybe within your congregation. Your small group is the ideal place to start developing such friendships. As weekly meetings proceed, friendships grow naturally and then will expand outward.

4. Encourage. In the early church, Barnabas and the apostles encouraged Paul. In response, Paul urged new Christians to "encourage one another and build up each other" (1 Thessalonians 5:11). In our modern society, negative criticism dominates our political and cultural environment, which often leads to fear, insecurity, trepidation, and timidity. People may shrivel up or close down in a too critical atmosphere, yet everyone can flourish in an atmosphere of encouragement. For example, you and your helpers should strive to find ways to affirm each participant each week.

There are many ways to encourage participants, especially those who are not part of your congregation. A key way of encouragement is for you to know everyone's name. Write down everyone's name at the first session, pray for the people by name each day during the week, and call each person by name during the second session. Throughout the program, smile at people and express warmth and responsiveness to every participant.

Encouragement also involves the gift of engaging others in conversation. Especially try to foster contributions from the quieter members of your group. If one person has done a lot of talking, ask, "What do the rest of you think?" In addition, ask simple, open-ended questions, such as, "What do you think?" and "How do you feel?" and "What has been your experience?" Good questions are open-ended ones that cannot be answered "Yes" or "No." Ask questions that provoke discussion, such as, "How does this story match your experiences?" As a small-group leader you typically should not answer your own questions; if people seem reluctant to answer, try rephrasing. If someone asks you a question that you cannot answer, be honest and say, "I don't know, but I will try to find out by next week."

Remember that all contributions by each member in your small group have value. Even when a group member says something that may appear wrong or silly, positive ways of responding might include, "How interesting!" or "That's a new idea I've never considered!" Create an environment in which group members can say what they think without fear of embarrassment or ridicule. Involving everyone means taking seriously the ideas, opinions, and insights of each person. Agreeing with other people or having people agree with you is not the goal or point.

Involvement, however, does not always require speaking. Some people actively participate simply by listening. Grant every person in your group the right to be silent or to say, "Pass" when a question is asked. Silence can be golden. Do not insist that introverts become extroverts. All of these techniques will result in a group that understands you as an encourager.

5. Listen. The Letter of James states, "Be quick to listen, slow to speak" (James 1:19). In your small group, speak softly and listen intently. If participants have ideas that are odd or strange, do not respond too quickly (as if their ideas are not even worth considering) or correct them. First, listen. Then try to understand the other persons' perspectives or feelings. Finally, show respect. Because listening is more important than speaking, you should not force your own ideas on the group. If someone directly asks you for your own view, answer briefly and then redirect the question to other participants.

6. Keep confidentiality. Assure the members of your small group that their personal stories or issues stay within the group. While your small group may not be bound by rules regarding pastoral confidentiality, gossip and inappropriate conversation outside the group will destroy relationships that are forming. At your first session, insist that people listen carefully to one another and then keep in confidence what is shared in the group. If you perceive that a participant has a particular need or is involved in a crisis, you may wish to share this concern with your pastor in a way that does not break confidence.

7. Be a peacemaker. Be gracious, and avoid getting into arguments. Encourage everyone to follow the old Southern phrase, "You do not have to like anyone, but you must be courteous to everyone." People rarely change their mind after they get involved in an argument, especially if the disagreement is about religion. It is easy to win an argument and lose a person. If an argument begins, quickly reconcile differences or acknowledge that there are different legitimate opinions. Tears, fears, and anger may all be part of this process; but neither you nor anyone else should dictate how other people respond. Truth is important, but speak the truth in love.

These seven positive qualities—patience, caring, building, encouraging, listening, keeping confidences, and peacemaking—will ensure your success as a small-group leader. When you exhibit these qualities, the way will be smooth.

There are a number of leadership skills that you will also use:

1. Be prepared. If you are not properly prepared, your discussion will flounder. Each week, review the material to be presented; read the appropriate chapter in *Beginnings: Along the Way: A Participant's Companion;* answer the questions for yourself; evaluate your own leadership the previous week; consider each participant and his or her own needs and expectations; and then be ready to lead.

2. Guide the conversation gently. For example, if a participant becomes too dominant, be willing, for the sake of the whole group, to intervene gently by saying, "What do others of you think?" or speak with the person after adjournment. Permitting one participant to dominate, for the sake of avoiding conflict, can have a harm-ful effect on the discussion. On the opposite side, if you are an excessively dominant leader, you may kill dialogue by doing all the talking instead of giving the participants the freedom to speak and to say what is on their mind. Do not see yourself as an expert with an appropriate response to whatever anyone says; that is, do not dominate the conversation. Silence is okay. In general, if you speak for more than five minutes of the discussion, you have spoken too much. Patience and listening are the needed skills.

3. Avoid fixing individual problems. When someone presents a specific problem to your group, it is tempting for you and others in the group to want to find a solution and fix the problem. Problem solving can make you and other people feel better, wiser, and more powerful; but fixing is not helping. Instead, share your own experiences and let the participants find their own solutions. Also, avoid attempting to convince everyone to follow someone else's personal path. It is far more useful to be able to clarify and celebrate someone's experience than to urge another person to try to duplicate another's unique experience.

4. Keep a sense of time. Watch the clock, and keep to the schedule. Keep your discussion to the set time. Also, make sure that your group does not spend too much time on a minor question and, as a result, have less time to spend on deeper questions that you know will arise later in the session. Finally, the session should not extend beyond the adjournment time, even if the group members are involved in a lively discussion. It is better to say, "Let's continue this next week," which will encourage people to return to continue the dialogue. The danger in going beyond the adjournment time is that some people may hesitate to come back, fearing another late adjournment. If persons wish to stay and continue the conversation, however, you and your helpers should make yourselves available until each participant is ready to leave.

5. Finally, the greatest gift you must have is the gift of prayer. Pray for your small group and for each participant every day. Begin this pattern at the end of your first discussion in the first week by closing the session with prayer. As the small-group leader, take the lead in this prayer, especially in the first few weeks. Your prayers should be brief. If you offer long, poetic prayers, this may hinder other people in the group from offering their own tentative prayers.

As the weeks pass, you may want to invite other members of your group to pray; but be careful not to put anyone on the spot. If you ask participants to pray, instead of asking them spontaneously in front of everyone else, ask them prior to the session so they will have a chance to prepare. If persons are not experienced in praying in public, you may suggest a simple prayer, such as, "Will you ask God to watch over us this next week?" Because many people find praying out loud very difficult, you may wish to introduce a simple model, such as, "Almighty God, (a short petition for each person in your group). We pray in Jesus' name. Amen." Be sensitive to people's feelings, and do not pressure anyone to pray aloud who does not want to do so.

In conclusion, as a small-group leader you need, and God will provide for you, a host of spiritual gifts and leadership skills. When you truly care for the participants and welcome all of them into your community through all your words and actions, God will change lives. Even more so, you who have befriended these persons will also be blessed by God. Leading people in their journey with Jesus Christ and watching them grow in their relationship with him are two of the highest joys of Christian faith.

SMALL-GROUP HELPERS

Every small group should also have one-to-three helpers with the same qualities and gifts as the small-group leaders.

Serving as a helper is the best way for a person to receive training to be a leadership team member and/or small-group leader the next time *Beginnings* is offered. There may be occasions when the small-group leader must miss a session or needs special help to bring a discussion back to focus. There may also be times when a group member needs some extra help. This will be the task of the small-group helpers.

If a small-group leader must miss a session and the small-group helper is asked to lead it, he or she needs to go over the general outline of the presentation and the discussion questions. The helper can draw on any particular knowledge he or she has about any of the participants that may be helpful but does not violate confidentiality. The small-group helper also needs to give special attention to preparation details such as set-up and closing prayer.

The use of small-group helpers solves one problem: persons who ask to come back and go through the program again. In many cases, rather than allowing persons to go through the program again, it is appropriate to ask them to come back as helpers. No one should simply repeat the program; people may get stuck going through *Beginnings* over and over again. Everyone needs to move on in the journey of faith. One excellent way to continue the spiritual journey is to come back and help others claim God's grace in their lives. People who have recently completed the program are often especially sensitive to the fears and doubts of members of the group they are serving as helpers. They can empathize with them, saying, "I understand that" or "I have that question too." This level of participation removes the barriers between "us" (the hosts) and "them" (the guests).

In addition to those people who request to come back, leadership team members of a previous program may recommend other people from their small group who would be good at helping. The final evaluation by small-group leaders (page 66) offers a way to recommend other persons for leadership positions.

Helpers must understand, however, that their role is to help, not to lead or dominate. Helpers, sometimes because of their own experiences, may wish to use the small group as a sounding board. Most of the conversation, however, must come from the participants, not from the small-group leaders and helpers. Helpers should resist the temptation to speak first or to speak often.

HELPING PARTICIPANTS
FOLLOW JESUS CHRIST

The most satisfying and terrifying moment for any leader and host of *Beginnings* is when a participant asks, "How can I become a Christian? How can I follow Jesus?" When a participant asks such questions, you have the opportunity to witness a new birth in Christ. These opportunities will come when you have trusting relationships with participants. When you express a clear, non-manipulative interest in a participant, not as a number but as a person, the conversation will get more serious. When participants see in you a lifestyle that is attractive, they will want to live that way themselves. In

Beginnings, participants watch their leaders every week —what they say, how they act, and where their loyalties lie. Participants who find your walk with Jesus Christ intriguing and compelling will want to go further. As your dialogue continues, you must be willing to offer Jesus Christ as the true guide. However you act, finally, you must be willing to let Jesus Christ through the Holy Spirit do the work. Jesus Christ is always knocking on the door; your job as a guide is to help other people hear the knock. Such a pattern of relational evangelism is faithful to our definition of evangelism, one beggar helping another beggar find food.

There are numerous biblical models of spiritual guides helping people hear God's voice and find the gospel feast. Jesus meeting the Samaritan woman at the well in John 4 is a story that can shape how we Christians may witness to our faith in God through Jesus Christ. In this biblical story, which we use in Session 2, Jesus met the woman where she was in her everyday life, drawing water from a well. Jesus paid particular attention to her as an individual, even though a Jewish man speaking to a Samaritan woman was contrary to popular custom. Jesus asked her for a drink of water, thus beginning a conversation with her about something much deeper: water that would quench her thirst forever. Through this conversation, the woman learned that Jesus was indeed the Messiah and could give her living water. This model of sharing the feast—meeting people where they are, caring for them as an individual, beginning a conversation, talking about deep subjects, challenging assumptions, and offering living water—is a wonderful illustration of how you may offer the life and hope of God through Jesus Christ to other people.

Another biblical model comes from the disciple Philip in Acts 8. *Beginnings* uses this illustration as the foundation for Session 6, which is about the Bible. Philip, one of the twelve disciples, was caught up in the activity of the post-Pentecost church in Jerusalem. Then, suddenly, the Holy Spirit led Philip away from his comfort zone to a wilderness road. Philip was willing to go where God wanted him to go. On this road, Philip discovered an inquirer, an Ethiopian official who was already reading God's holy word from the Book of Isaiah. The literal and spiritual journey of the Ethiopian had clearly already begun before Philip's arrival on the scene. Philip simply appeared, felt confident enough to introduce himself to this official, and was knowledgeable enough to answer his questions. But more than just answering questions, Philip was prepared to tell the story of Jesus. Philip clearly knew the Scriptures and was willing to share his journey with Jesus. When the Ethiopian asked for more, Philip provided more. And when the Ethiopian came to a point of decision, Philip was even willing to baptize him in the wilderness.

Most people come to Jesus Christ in private, intimate ways through conversations like these in John 4 and Acts 8. At the end of Chapter 7 in the book *Beginnings: Along the Way: A Participant's Companion*, we also describe a few basic steps that are part of making a decision for Jesus Christ. This chapter, especially at its conclusion, offers participants an opportunity to respond to the gift of life Jesus Christ offers. All your leadership team members need to be aware of and supportive of this kind of response. In Chapter 12, we also offer other ways for persons to share their faith. In that chapter we encourage participants to be willing to share what they have discovered with others. The suggestions are also appropriate for all the members of your leadership team. The following is an excerpt from the material at the end of Chapter 7 and in *Beginnings: Participant's Guide*.

HOW CAN I BEGIN AN INTENTIONAL JOURNEY WITH JESUS CHRIST?

How Can I Become a Christian?

Being a Christian means following Jesus Christ. How does that happen? Do you remember the inquirer in our first session, Nicodemus? Nicodemus was a good man who was looking for the meaning of life. Nicodemus probably fasted twice a week, prayed in the Temple in Jerusalem, gave his money away generously, and even taught religion at the religious academy. Yet with all these good deeds, he was still looking for direction in his journey. Jesus said to Nicodemus, "You must be born from above" (John 3:7).

Because from the moment of birth all human beings are on a spiritual journey, the question is not, "When will you begin your walk with Jesus Christ?" Jesus Christ has always been walking beside you. Rather, the major question is, "Are you ready to begin an intentional, deliberate, and disciplined journey with Jesus Christ?" You have to choose which road to travel. Christians are the people who choose to walk along the way with Jesus Christ. How do you decide? How can you begin?

For each person, the answer is different. In the New Testament and throughout history, each of Jesus' followers came to him differently. Stories of redirection toward Jesus often have more differences than similarities. There is no simple formula, no cookie cutter recipe, no one road map, and no magic words. But all Christians have made a choice to follow Jesus Christ.

Can you choose to follow Jesus Christ today? Of course you can. Should you choose today? That is for you to decide. But if you want to walk down Jesus' path, one way to go is simply to say several very simple words to Jesus Christ. They begin as follows:

1. "Thank you God" for your love. Jesus said to Nicodemus, "God so loved the world that God gave God's only Son, so that everyone who believes in Jesus Christ may not perish but may have eternal life" (John 3:16; author's translation). You too have to acknowledge God as your loving Parent. Open your eyes, ears, and heart to see Jesus Christ coming to you and embracing you.

2. "I'm sorry" that I have not been following your way. Jesus began his ministry by telling everyone, "Turn around and believe in the good news" (Mark 1:15). If you have been walking down another road, you must admit that you have not been walking with Jesus Christ.

3. "Redirect me," and help me follow Jesus Christ in every step I take. As Peter, another New Testament writer said, "Follow in his [Jesus'] steps" (1 Peter 2:21) and "For you were going astray like sheep, but now you have returned to the shepherd" (1 Peter 2:25). Say to Jesus Christ, "Jesus, be my companion and guide; point me in the right direction."

4. "Let's start" the journey today. As Paul said to some early Christians, "Now is the day of salvation" (2 Corinthians 6:2). Jesus Christ can become your guide today. "If you confess with your lips that Jesus is Lord and believe in your heart that God raised him [Jesus] from the dead, you will be saved" (Romans 10:9). You may choose a new road to travel right now.

It is that simple.

These four phrases—Thank you, I'm sorry, redirect me, let's start—may take the form of a private conversation with God, such as,

"O loving God, I'm sorry about the roads I have traveled. I want to travel with Jesus today. Amen."
or
"Almighty God, I've made some wrong turns and am far from where I need to be. Jesus, guide me now. Amen."
or
"Jesus, I'm sorry. Why don't you take over now? Amen.

These four steps may also take place during a conversation with a Christian friend or another participant in or leader of *Beginnings*. There are people around you in this program who would love to talk with you about following Jesus Christ. Just ask someone you trust.

Meeting Jesus Christ requires making room for him in your life and claiming him as your guide and shepherd along the way. Jesus Christ always comes to you. The appropriate response at each moment is to go to him. Despite your doubts, your fears, your denials, you simply have to say "Yes" to Jesus Christ. This new relationship depends on your listening, repenting, and trusting and on being empowered by Jesus Christ. As Jesus told his disciples, "I do not call you servants . . . but I have called you friends" (John 15:15).

For some further reading about how to assist people in their journey, see *The Faith-Sharing New Testament With the Psalms,* by Eddie Fox and George Morris (Cokesbury in cooperation with Thomas Nelson, 1994). This book provides some additional resources about how to be a faithful companion to people considering becoming intentional Christians. Being a spiritual guide for a new birth is one of the highest privileges of being a follower of Jesus Christ. As a leadership team member you must not back away from such an opportunity but claim it as a gift from God.

SUMMARY

The small group, the heart of *Beginnings*, brings participants into relationship with one another; with your congregation as a whole; and, most importantly, with Jesus Christ. These small groups serve as the catalyst to fundamental Christian formation. While no one comes to *Beginnings* specifically to be in a small group, by the end of the program all participants will discover that being part of a small group is a critical aspect of finding their way to Jesus Christ.

1. From *A Generation of Seekers,* by Wade Clark Roof (HarperSanFrancisco, 1993); page 252.

8.
Additional Resources

The following resources in print have good practical advice and/or theological background that may be used by leadership team members for further help and information:

Barna, G. *Re-Churching the Unchurched*. Barna: California, 2000. A basic book of sociological research about the unchurched in North America.

Bertodono, Teresa De. *Soul Searchers: An Anthology of Spiritual Journeys*. Eerdmans: Grand Rapids, 2001. A collection of writings by pilgrims and travelers.

Brouwer, D.J. *Remembering the Faith: What Christians Believe*. Eerdmans: Grand Rapids, 1999. A conservative description of the Christian faith.

CHRISTIAN BELIEVER. United Methodist Publishing House: Nashville. A thirty-week survey of basic Christian doctrine.

"Christian Initiation Series," a series of books by the General Board of Discipleship of The United Methodist Church that helps "congregations as they create settings where seekers can discover God's welcome and participate in an accompanied journey that brings them to the waters of baptism, life in the church, and discipleship in daily life."

Collins, K. J. & Tyson, J. H. *Conversion in the Wesleyan Tradition*. Abingdon Press: Nashville, 2001. A survey of Arminian perspectives on Christian conversion by a variety of authors.

Dunham, Maxie. *This Is Christianity*. Abingdon Press: Nashville, 1994. A primer about Christianity based on the Apostles' Creed.

Evans, C. Stephen. *Why Believe?: Reason and Mystery as Pointers to God*. Eerdmans: Grand Rapids, 1996. Apologetics from a conservative, Reformed perspective.

Fiddes, Paul S. *Participating in God: A Pastoral Doctrine of the Trinity*. Westminster John Knox Press: Louisville, 2000. This book develops an understanding of the Trinity in conversation with the human experiences of suffering, death, and forgiveness.

"Foundations of Christian Faith" series by the Presbyterian Church, U.S.A. A series of accessible books about theological issues for serious Christians and persons on the edge of faith.

Fox, H.E. & Morris, G.E. *Faith-Sharing*. Discipleship Resources: Nashville, 1986. A workbook on how to encourage laity to share their faith. See also *The Faith-Sharing New Testament With Psalms* by Fox and Morris that gives additional insights to faith sharing by laypersons.

Fuller, Robert C. *Spiritual, But Not Religious: Understanding Unchurched America*. Oxford University Press: Oxford, 2002. Another survey of the diversity of spiritual longing in North America.

Green, Michael. *Evangelism Through the Local Church*. Thomas Nelson: Nashville, 1992. A classic book by an English Anglican scholar that covers the whole spectrum of evangelism, both theology and practice.

Hall, Douglas John. *Why Christian? For Those on the Edge of Faith*. Fortress Press: Minneapolis, 1998. Hall addresses the predominant questions of young adult inquirers "on the edge" of making a commitment to Christianity. Appropriate for beginners in the faith, Hall avoids the temptation to oversimplify Christian beliefs or to rush toward persuasion.

Harrington, P. *10 FAQs of New Christians*. Discipleship Resources: Nashville, 2000. Simple answers to ten "frequently asked questions" by seekers.

Johnson, B.C. *A Seeker's Guide to Christian Faith*. Upper Room: Nashville, 2000. A personal workbook introducing an individual to Jesus.

Johnson, Luke Timothy. *Living Jesus: Learning the Heart of the Gospel*. Harper: New York, 1999. A clearly written account of the meaning of the Resurrection; offers a compelling reflection on the mystery of Christ's presence today.

Kerr, H.T. & Mulder, J.M. *Conversions*. Eerdmans: Grand Rapids, 1983. A classic survey of conversion narratives.

Lindvall, Michael L. *The Christian Life: A Geography of God*. Geneva Press: Louisville, 2001. One of a series of books, this one about journey as a spiritual metaphor, for laypersons about theological issues.

Milton, Ralph. *Christianity for Beginners*. Abingdon: Nashville, 1998. A book by a Canadian that introduces basic Christian theology.

Morris, George E. *The Mystery and Meaning of Christian Conversion*. Discipleship Resources: Nashville, 1981. A foundational introduction to conversion, particularly from a Wesleyan perspective.

Pawlowsky, P. *Christianity: The Basics*. SCM Trinity Press: Valley Forge, 1994. A conservative introduction to basic beliefs.

Placher, William C. *Jesus the Savior: The Meaning of Jesus Christ for Christian Faith*. Westminster John Knox Press: Louisville, 2001. Provides both an engaging portrait of the life of Jesus and a cogent explanation of Christian beliefs concerning Jesus.

Roof, Wade Clark. *A Generation of Seekers*. HarperSanFrancisco, 1993. A classic book about the spiritual needs of the baby-boomer generation.

Stott, John R. W. *Basic Christianity*. Inter-Varsity Press: Downers Grove, Illinois, 1971. A classic, conservative affirmation of the essential affirmations of orthodox Christianity.

Strobel, L. *Inside the Mind of Unchurched Harry and Mary*. Zondervan: Grand Rapids, 1993. A wonderful introduction to persons outside the institutional church.

Taylor, Barbara Brown. *Speaking of Sin: The Lost Language of Salvation*. Cowley Publications: Cambridge, 2000. A highly readable perspective on human sin seen within the context of salvation.

Webber, Robert E. *Journey to Jesus: The Worship, Evangelism, and Nurture Mission of the Church*. Abingdon: Nashville, 2001. A contemporary interpretation of how to integrate evangelism with the worship ministry of a congregation.

Wilmoth, R.E. *How United Methodists Share Their Faith*. Abingdon: Nashville, 1999. A nonjudgmental, sensitive, listening style of evangelism.

Wuthnow, Robert. *Christianity in the 21st Century: Reflections on the Challenges Ahead*. Oxford University Press, New York. 1993. An American sociologist and religious historian charts the major issues facing Christians in the new millennium.

Yancey, Philip. *Reaching for the Invisible God: What Can We Expect to Find?* Zondervan: Grand Rapids, Michigan, 2000. A highly readable account of our human search for God; creatively portrays the nature of God's identity and relationship to us.

Yancey, Philip. *The Jesus I Never Knew*. Zondervan: Grand Rapids, Michigan, 1995. Yancey challenges many of the common assumptions of who Jesus is and offers a renewed perspective drawn from a creative reading of the Gospels.

In addition, there are many other resources in the area of apologetics that are out of print. A survey of libraries and bookshelves will reveal many additional resources.

9.
Reproducible Forms

The following pages may be reproduced for use in your local congregation.

BEGINNINGS REGISTRATION FORM

Name: _____

Address: _____

Phone: _____

E-mail: _____

Childcare: Yes_   No_

Ages/Names of children: _____

Special Diet Requirements: _____

The following **optional** *information will help us determine the right small group for you:*

Age: _____

Gender: _____

Profession: _____

Marital Status: _____

Will you attend with a spouse or friend?   Yes_   No_

Their name: _____

BEGINNINGS REGISTRATION FORM

Name: _____

Address: _____

Phone: _____

E-mail: _____

Childcare: Yes_   No_

Ages/Names of children: _____

Special Diet Requirements: _____

The following **optional** *information will help us determine the right small group for you:*

Age: _____

Gender: _____

Profession: _____

Marital Status: _____

Will you attend with a spouse or friend?   Yes_   No_

Their name: _____

BEGINNINGS: AN INTRODUCTION TO CHRISTIAN FAITH

We invite you to join a new *Beginnings* program.
September 10th–November 5th
Nine weeks on Wednesday evenings at Central United Methodist Church.
5:30 PM to 7:30 PM

Each session includes a meal, a presentation about basic Christian beliefs, and small discussion groups.
Special Day Apart retreat on October 18th.

Ideal for anyone who wants to learn more about the Christian faith.
Wonderful opportunity to meet new people and make new friends.

Free childcare.

The meal and program are offered without cost to guests.
For more information, call xxx-xxx-xxxx or check www.xxxx.

- -

BEGINNINGS: AN INTRODUCTION TO CHRISTIAN FAITH

We invite you to join a new *Beginnings* program.
Date:_____
Where:_____
When:_____

Each session includes a meal, a presentation about basic Christian beliefs, and small discussion groups.
Special Day Apart retreat on _____.

Ideal for anyone who wants to learn more about the Christian faith.
Wonderful opportunity to meet new people and make new friends.

Free childcare.

The meal and program are offered without cost to guests.
For more information, call _____or check www._____.

BEGINNINGS SCHEDULE

Date:_____ Session 1: **So, Is This All There Is?**

Date:_____ Session 2: **Who Is Jesus, and Why Should I Care?**

Date:_____ Session 3: **Why Am I Not Where I Want to Be?**

Date:_____ Session 4: **What Happens When I Die?**

Date:_____ Session 5: **Can I Trust God?**

Date:_____ Session 6: **How Does God Speak to Me?**

Date:_____ ("Day Apart" or three additional dates)

Date:_____ Session 7: **If I Don't Feel Lost, Why Do I Need to Be Found?**

Date:_____ Session 8: **Can I Start Again?**

Date:_____ Session 9: **How Do I Speak to God?**

Date:_____ Session 10: **How Can I Make a Life and Not Just a Living?**

Date:_____ Session 11: **Why Should I Join Any Group That Will Have Me as a Member?**

Date:_____ Session 12: **Love Feast!**

- -

BEGINNINGS SCHEDULE

Date:_____ Session 1: **So, Is This All There Is?**

Date:_____ Session 2: **Who Is Jesus, and Why Should I Care?**

Date:_____ Session 3: **Why Am I Not Where I Want to Be?**

Date:_____ Session 4: **What Happens When I Die?**

Date:_____ Session 5: **Can I Trust God?**

Date:_____ Session 6: **How Does God Speak to Me?**

Date:_____ ("Day Apart" or three additional dates)

Date:_____ Session 7: **If I Don't Feel Lost, Why Do I Need to Be Found?**

Date:_____ Session 8: **Can I Start Again?**

Date:_____ Session 9: **How Do I Speak to God?**

Date:_____ Session 10: **How Can I Make a Life and Not Just a Living?**

Date:_____ Session 11: **Why Should I Join Any Group That Will Have Me as a Member?**

Date:_____ Session 12: **Love Feast!**

BEGINNINGS CONTACT SHEET

The following information will not be shared with members of the group or used to contact you except under special circumstances, such as the need to cancel a session or to alert persons about a problem.

Small Group:

Name _____ Phone Number _____ E-mail _____

Name _____ Phone Number _____ E-mail _____

Name _____ Phone Number _____ E-mail _____

Name _____ Phone Number _____ E-mail _____

Name _____ Phone Number _____ E-mail _____

Name _____ Phone Number _____ E-mail _____

Name _____ Phone Number _____ E-mail _____

Name _____ Phone Number _____ E-mail _____

Name _____ Phone Number _____ E-mail _____

Name _____ Phone Number _____ E-mail _____

Name _____ Phone Number _____ E-mail _____

Name _____ Phone Number _____ E-mail _____

Name _____ Phone Number _____ E-mail _____

BEGINNINGS DAY APART REGISTRATION FORM

We will be gathering on Saturday, October 18, for our Day Apart retreat. We will gather at the Shalom Center at 100 W. Trade Street at 8:30 AM and continue until 4:00 PM. We will begin with a light breakfast. Lunch will be served. Childcare will be offered throughout the day on site. On this day, we will cover three of the most important sessions of *Beginnings*. This is a day not to miss. Below is the schedule for the day. Please register for this day as soon as possible and give to your small-group leader.

Schedule:

8:00 AM	Leaders and Helpers Arrive and Set Out Breakfast Snacks
8:30 AM	Participants Arrive
9:00 AM	Introduction to the Day and Gathering Songs (optional)
9:20 AM	Video/DVD Presentation 7: If I Don't Feel Lost, Why Do I Need to Be Found? Salvation and Conversion
9:40 AM	Refreshment Break
10:00 AM	Discussion
10:50 AM	Break
11:00 AM	Introduction to Video/DVD Presentation 8
11:05 AM	Video/DVD Presentation 8: Can I Start Again? Forgiveness and Wholeness
11:25 AM	Discussion
12:00 noon	Break
12:15 PM	Lunch and Continuing Group Discussion
1:00 PM	Free Time for Walk or Conversations
1:30 PM	Introduction to Video/DVD Presentation 9
1:35 PM	Video/DVD Presentation 9: How Do I Speak to God? Prayer
1:50 PM	Discussion
2:30 PM	Break
2:45 PM	Large Group Worship (Possibly Including Holy Communion)
3:45 PM	Adjourn

Registration:

Name:

Childcare: Yes_ No_   Ages/Names of children:

Special Diet Requirements:

Would you be interested in supper on this day?   Yes___ No____

You Are Invited to a Love Feast

We invite you to a Love Feast.

Place:_____

Day:_____

Date:_____

Time:_____

Our Love Feast includes a free meal, a review of our journey together in *Beginnings,* and some friendly conversation for participants in *Beginnings* along with their families and friends.

Free childcare.
No offering will be received.

For more information call_____, or email_____

BEGINNINGS LOVE FEAST REGISTRATION FORM

Name:_____

Childcare: Yes____ No____

Ages/Names of children:_____

Special Diet Requirements:_____

Number of family and friends attending:_____

BEGINNINGS PARTICIPANT QUESTIONNAIRE
(Please turn in today or no later than next week.)

Name_____

Small Group_____

1. How did you learn about *Beginnings*?

2. Why did you decide to attend*?*

3. How did you benefit from *Beginnings*?

4. What did you enjoy most about *Beginnings?*

5. What did you find most difficult?

6. How could the program be improved?

7. Other comments:

8. Are you willing to assist in a future *Beginnings* program?

BEGINNINGS *SMALL-GROUP LEADER QUESTIONNAIRE*
(Please turn in today or no later than next week.)

Name_____

Small Group_____

1. How did you become a small-group leader?

2. How did you benefit from *Beginnings*?

3. What did you find most difficult?

4. How could the program be improved?

5. Other comments:

6. Are you willing to be a small-group leader the next time the program is offered?

   Yes____No____How_____

SMALL-GROUP LEADER EVALUATION OF PARTICIPANTS

Describe your group members, including: level of participation, next steps in their spiritual journey, ability to offer a testimony at the Love Feast, and possibility of becoming a helper the next time the program is offered.

Name_____

Completed course? Y____ N____

If not, do you know why? _____

Able to offer witness at Love Feast? Y____ N____

Possible helper in a future program? Y____ N____

Other comments: _____

(Repeat/continue for each participant)

- -

SMALL-GROUP LEADER EVALUATION OF PARTICIPANTS

Describe your group members, including: level of participation, next steps in their spiritual journey, ability to offer a testimony at the Love Feast, and possibility of becoming a helper the next time the program is offered.

Name_____

Completed course? Y____ N____

If not, do you know why? _____

Able to offer witness at Love Feast? Y____ N____

Possible helper in a future program? Y____ N____

Other comments: _____

(Repeat/continue for each participant)

10.
Meals

The following suggestions for meals are not listed in any particular order; they are simply a list of options that your meal coordinator may consider. The following menu options are for approximately ten persons; adjust the amount of the ingredients based on the size of the group. Also review the meal and snack suggestions found on page 38.

Greek Chicken

A meal with tomatoes, dried mint, red pepper, parsley, yellow pepper, black pepper, feta cheese, olive oil, oregano, and boneless chicken breasts. Dice tomatoes and peppers; combine with remaining ingredients except chicken and oil. Grease dish and place chicken in dish. Top with mixture. Drizzle with oil and bake at 350 degrees for 30 minutes. Serve with salad and bread.

Grilled Cheese and Tomato Soup

Make an average of two grilled cheese sandwiches per person and 8 ounces of soup per person. One gallon of soup will be enough for sixteen persons to have extra. For an appetizer, prepare raw vegetables (carrots, broccoli, celery, cauliflower cut into bite-size pieces) with a dip on the side. Make a simple dip with sour cream and powdered onion soup.

Cajun Chicken Pasta

Sauté in butter sliced boneless chicken breasts, mushrooms, green bell peppers, and onions until done. Heat fresh cream and add Cajun spices. Mix everything with cooked linguini pasta and top with Parmesan cheese.

Lasagna

Many grocery stores sell family-size frozen lasagna that serves twelve people. The lasagna comes in two varieties: meat sauce and vegetarian. Tossed Salad with lettuce and fresh vegetables. Two-to-three bottles of salad dressing (Ranch, Italian, Honey Mustard, and French). Italian bread or buttered toast.

BBQ Chicken Pizza

Toss cooked chicken, honey mustard BBQ sauce, red onion, sun-dried tomatoes, and mushrooms together. Spoon on pizza shell and top with mozzarella cheese. Bake until cheese is bubbling.

Take-Out

Call out for pizza, deli sandwiches, chicken, and/or BBQ. Look for specials and vegetarian and low-calorie options. With pizza, order a few with cheese or vegetarian toppings, averaging one large pizza for every three people. For this meal, make sure that someone picks up the food rather than anxiously waiting for delivery.

Special Chicken

Sauté boneless chicken breasts and place in dish. Top with cooked bacon and shredded Monterey Jack cheese. Melt cheese in oven. Serve with honey mustard sauce.

Make Your Own Sandwich

Have assorted breads and rolls. Provide Pimento cheese for vegetarians. On the side have ham, turkey, and roast beef; Swiss and American cheese; lettuce, tomato, and pickles; mustard and mayonnaise; potato chips and other chips.

Spinach-Stuffed Lasagna Ruffles

Blend cream cheese, spinach, ricotta, mozzarella, Parmesan, and Italian seasonings. Spread spinach mixture on cooked lasagna noodles and roll up. Place noodles in a dish and top with spaghetti sauce and more mozzarella. Serve with salad and bread.

Baked Potato Bar

Wash the potatoes and wrap in aluminum foil, shiny side on the inside; or bake the potatoes without foil, which results in crisper skins. On the table have butter and margarine, sour cream, bacon bits, and mushrooms (cleaned and sliced), plus grated cheese and anything else you like.

Kung Pao Pork/Chicken

Combine boneless pork loin or chicken, soy sauce, garlic, sugar, red pepper, lemon juice, onion, cornstarch, peanuts, crushed red pepper in a wok or pan and sauté. Serve with rice.

Chili and Cornbread

Invite someone from Texas to share an old family recipe. On the side have grated cheese, chopped onions, sour cream, and crackers. For cornbread, use a prepared cornbread mix and follow directions on box.

Chicken Salad on Croissants

Combine diced, cooked chicken; grapes; apples; and walnuts in a bowl. Combine sugar, mayonnaise, sour cream, and lemon juice. Stir into chicken mixture. Serve on croissants with chips and fruit.

Hot Dogs

Serve two hot dogs per person. (And yes, there are vegetarian hot dogs out there.) On the side have chips, rolls (Their number will never equal the number of hot dogs in a pack.), ketchup, mustard, chopped onions, slaw, and chili.

Vegetarian Tortellini

Sauté green peppers and onions in oil. Add canned diced tomatoes. Cook tortellini and drain. Serve with tomato mixture on top. Serve with salad and bread.

Spaghetti

Find someone from Italy who has an old family recipe to share. Make a tossed salad and serve with buttered toast or garlic bread.

Chicken Wraps

Combine cooked chicken, chopped apple, cucumber, onion, and green pepper and stir in yogurt. Place same mixture on flour tortilla and roll up. Serve with chips and baby carrots.

Tacos

Provide three taco shells per person, soft or hard. On the side have mild or hot taco seasoning in the jar, grated cheese, shredded lettuce, chopped tomato, sour cream, olives, and taco sauce. A variation of this meal could be a taco salad meal.

Quesadilla

Top flour tortilla with desired ingredients; then place another tortilla on top. Ingredients may include cooked chicken, fresh baby spinach, sauteed mushrooms, black beans (drained), Monterey Jack cheese, shredded feta cheese, or whatever you can find. Grill tortillas in a frying pan. Cut into wedges. Serve with yellow rice.

Breakfast (People love breakfast at night!)

Prepare eggs, bacon, toast, and tatter tots. On the side have a variety of fresh fruit or pastries. Pancakes and waffles add a festive atmosphere. Orange juice and coffee.

Burritos

Heat flour tortilla and top with cooked chicken, cooked rice, black beans, onions, green pepper, olives, sour cream, and salsa. Fold to close. Serve with tortilla chips and salsa.

Chicken Stir-fry

Prepare fresh chicken and vegetables, and serve with steamed or fried rice. For fun, instead of providing forks, encourage everyone to use chopsticks.

Circle Salad

Sauté chopped walnuts and noodles in butter. Drain. Combine oil, sugar, soy sauce, and red wine vinegar in a jar and shake. Combine chopped, cooked chicken; lettuce; broccoli; onions; walnuts; and noodles. Top with dressing. Serve with bread.

Italian Sausage Subs

Cook the sausage and serve on sliced sub rolls. Also have some prepared pizza sauce and grated mozzarella cheese on the side, and have lots of napkins.

While all the above meals are simple, your meal coordinator may dress up each meal in creative ways. For example, wear a cowboy hat when serving chili, a baseball cap while preparing hot dogs, or pajamas when serving the breakfast meal. Add a few flourishes like checkered tablecloths and candles in wine bottles while serving spaghetti, play country music while serving chili, or play Mexican music while serving tacos. Make the mealtime a fun experience for everyone.

Part Two:

Training Session Outlines

This section provides you with the necessary planning for each of two sessions to train those people who will lead the program in your congregation.

Training the Leadership Team

The director conducts leadership training for *Beginnings: An Introduction to Christian Faith*. It is vital to train all the members of your leadership team—small-group leaders, helpers, and support group members—at these two training sessions. These training sessions are usually held two weeks and one week in advance of the beginning of the actual program. If there is just one small group of participants in the program, all of this training may take place in one extended session. The training sessions follow the same outline as a *Beginnings* session: meal, possible singing, presentation, discussion. The first training session focuses on the goals of the program (See Chapters 1, 2, and 3 in this book.) and the leadership of small groups (See Chapter 7.). The second training session focuses on assignments and housekeeping details (See Chapters 4, 5, and 6.). You may also need to have a training session later in the program to plan the Day Apart retreat and the final Love Feast (See these details in Part Three.).

The following is a suggested training schedule for an evening. If you hold your training at another time, follow the same pattern.

5:00 PM	Trainers' Orientation and Prayer
5:15 PM	Team Members Begin to Gather
5:25 PM	Leader Orientation Ends
5:30 PM	Supper by Meal Coordinator
6:00 PM	Welcome by Director
6:10 PM	Worship Led by Music/Worship Leader (optional)
6:20 PM	Presentation (Week 1: Goals; Week 2: Assignments)
6:50 PM	Group Discussion
7:25 PM	Closing and Prayer
7:30 PM	Adjournment

The training sessions begin at 5:00 PM with an orientation for those persons who will lead this session, followed at 5:30 PM by supper. During the meal, the members of your leadership team visit with one another. At 6:00 PM you, as the director, introduce everyone and indicate each person's specific responsibility. Do not assume that all your leadership team members already know one another. At 6:10 PM the music/worship leader possibly continues the training with singing and prayer for ten minutes. You, as the director, then present the material for the evening, essentially outlining the content of the chapters of this resource and adding any particular emphases. After the presentation, anyone may ask questions relating to the content. When those fundamental questions are answered, entertain questions about any other aspect of the program. Your team, however, must understand that everyone must be willing to do anything from greeting at the door to washing dishes. Finally, throughout the training stress the importance of praying for the leadership team, for all the participants, and for the program. Finish each training session at 7:30 PM.

Training Session 1:
Introduction to *Beginnings*

INTRODUCTION

Group building and laying the foundations for *Beginnings*

PREPARATION *(everyone)*

Prepare yourself spiritually. Pray for yourself, the members of the leadership team, and all the participants. Review and outline Chapters 1, 2, and 3 of this book. See pages 27–30 in *Beginnings: Small-Group Leader's Guide*, which cover this training session. Encourage leadership team members to follow along in their individual copies of that book.

Make sure nametags for your team members are out and direction signs are up.

Check the sound system if you have more than twenty-four team members.

WELCOME *(10 minutes by director)*

Welcome everyone.

Introduce the members of the leadership team.

Ask people to introduce themselves to two persons they do not know and tell them one interesting fact about themselves.

Share any housekeeping details necessary for the first training session.

Identify the focus of this session: "Today, as we build our team, we will focus on why we will host *Beginnings* in our church and how we are expected to lead it."

SINGING

(optional; 10 minutes by music/worship leader)

TRAINING PRESENTATION 1
(30 minutes by director)

Present the information in Chapters 1, 2, and 3 in this book, which are about the program, the audience, and the goal of this program, and in Chapter 7, which is about the role of small groups in this program. See pages 27–30 in *Beginnings: Small-Group Leader's Guide*, which cover this first training session. Encourage leadership team members to follow along in their individual copies of that book. Mark your own emphases, and share them with your team.

DISCUSSION *(35 minutes guided by director)*

Answer questions, and attend to housekeeping details.

CLOSING *(5 minutes by director)*

Remind everyone about the schedule for next week, and make other necessary announcements.

Say everyone's name out loud.

Invite the group to pause for a minute of silence to reflect on this session.

Pray together.

Adjourn on time.

Training Session 2:
Preparing for *Beginnings*

INTRODUCTION

Group building and taking care of the housekeeping details that will make *Beginnings* successful

PREPARATION *(everyone)*

Prepare yourself spiritually. Pray for yourself, for the members of the leadership team, and for all the participants.

Review these leader's notes; Chapters 4, 5, and 6 in this book; and the material near the end of Chapter 7 about helping participants follow Jesus Christ. See pages 31–36 in *Beginnings: Small-Group Leader's Guide*, which cover this second training session. Encourage leadership team members to follow along in their individual copies of that book.

Make sure nametags are out and direction signs are up.

Check the sound system.

WELCOME *(5 minutes by director)*

Welcome all participants.

Ask participants to share one hope they have for this program.

Share any housekeeping details for this training session.

Identify the focus of this session: "Today, we will continue our team building by focusing on our responsibilities for this program."

SINGING
(optional; 10 minutes by music/worship leader)

TRAINING PRESENTATION 2
(30 minutes by director, music/worship leader, treasurer, meal coordinator)

Present the material in Chapters 4, 5, and 6 in this book and the material near the end of Chapter 7 about helping participants follow Jesus Christ. See pages 31–36 in *Beginnings: Small-Group Leader's Guide*, which cover this second training session. Encourage leadership team members to follow along in their individual copies of that book. Outline this material for your leadership team, and present your own emphases.

DISCUSSION *(35 minutes guided by director, music/worship leader, treasurer, meal coordinator)*

Answer questions, and attend to any final housekeeping details.

CLOSING *(5 minutes by director)*

Remind everyone about the schedule for next week, and make other necessary announcements.

Invite the group to pause for a minute of silence to reflect on this session.

Pray together.

Adjourn on time.

Part Three:

Session Outlines for Director

This section provides you with the detailed guidance to plan and lead each weekly session.

Session 1:
So, Is This All There Is?

Introduction

INTRODUCTION

All people are searching for meaning in their lives. We wonder why we are here, what our purpose is, where we can find guidance. Followers of Jesus believe that in our spiritual journey, Christ is the one who provides a solution to the problem of the restlessness in our lives and accompanies us on our journey. We invite you to join us in the journey to find answers to our most important questions.

PREPARATION

Prepare yourself spiritually. Pray for yourself and for all the participants.

Review these director's notes.

Read Chapter 1 in *Beginnings: Along the Way: A Participant's Companion*.

Watch the video/DVD presentation.

Prepare the gathering space.

Prepare the areas where the small group will meet. Provide copies of *Beginnings: Participant's Guide*, pencils/pens, and Bibles.

Check the TV and the VCR/DVD player, and cue the video/DVD.

Make sure nametags are out and direction signs are up.

Check the sound system.

Make copies of your *Beginnings* schedule (see page 60) and place on registration table.

OPENING HOSPITALITY

The first session is the most important session. Participants will get a feel for the entire program based on what happens when they walk in for the first time. The members of your leadership team should be the first people participants see. Your host pastor and every member of the leadership team, except small-group leaders, should serve as greeters. Guests often arrive with preconceived ideas of what Christians are like— boring, dry, and religious—so when guests are greeted by a normal, friendly person, they may be surprised. Be friendly, but not overly eager, as aggressive hospitality may overwhelm guests at the first session. First impressions are very important.

Helpers at the registration table need an alphabetical list of every participant, along with the names of your small-group leaders. Helpers also need to know where the groups will be seated for the meal. Quickly register walk-in participants (using the registration form on page 58), and assign them to an appropriate small group. Small-group leaders should not greet participants at the door but stay at their assigned meal table to greet members of their small group and to introduce small-group members to one another.

SERVE THE MEAL

WELCOME (5 minutes by director)

Welcome all participants.

Introduce group leaders.

Ask participants to introduce themselves to persons at their dinner/lunch table by telling one important thing about themselves that no one at the table knows.

Share any housekeeping details. Pass out contact sheets to small-group leaders.

State the focus of this session: "Today, we will hear the story of Nicodemus, a man who was searching for direction and meaning in his life. You may read the introduction to his story in your *Participant's Guide*" [or you, the director, may read John 3:1-3a aloud for everyone to hear].

SINGING
(optional; 5 minutes by music/worship leader)

VIDEO/DVD PRESENTATION 1 *(20 minutes)*

Start the video/DVD on time.

DISCUSSION *(45 minutes by small-group leader)*

Greet the participants again and distribute *Beginnings: Participant's Guide* and pencils/pens.

Speak about the issue of confidentiality. Remind everyone that what is shared in the small group should stay in the small group.

Group Questions

If your house were burning down and all your family and pets were safe and you only had time to save one item (no matter how difficult it would be to move it), what would you save? Why?

A lot of people sum up their basic approach to life on the bumper stickers they place on their cars:

"Normal People Worry Me"
"My Karma Ran Over Your Dogma"
"Money Isn't Everything ... But It Sure Keeps the Kids in Touch"
"Compost Happens"
"It's as Bad as You Think and They Are Out to Get You"

If you were to create your own bumper sticker, what would it say? How would it reflect your philosophy of life?

Rob described one of his earliest disappointments in life, the time he ordered "sea monkeys" from the back page of a comic book. Can you remember a time as a child when you were really excited about something—a toy, an event, or an experience—only to wonder later, "So, is this all there is?" Can you recall a more recent experience that made you ask this same question? If so, what happened?

Did you hear anything else from Rob that connects with your life? If so, what?

Personal Questions

Can you identify with Nicodemus looking for Jesus at night? Why or why not? What would his friends have said if they had known he had gone to visit with Jesus?

What would your family and friends say if they knew you were participating in *Beginnings*?

Do you believe that this is all there is? Is your heart satisfied or restless with the answers you've come up with so far?

✱ What do you hope to learn through participating in *Beginnings*? *(Privately fill out card)*

Can you remember a significant time of yearning to experience God? If so, where were you? How did you respond? Did you try to forget it? Did you feel unnerved? Did you embrace the yearning? Do you now have a yearning to know more about God?

CLOSING *(5 minutes by small-group leader)*

Remind everyone about the schedule for next week, and make other necessary announcements.

Pass around the contact form for the first time (see page 61). Remind participants that this information will be used only under special circumstances.

Invite the participants to pause for a minute of silence to reflect on this session.

Pray together.

Adjourn on time.

SPECIAL NOTE

After the participants have left, meet with the members of your leadership team briefly to review the first session and to identify any corrections you need to make for the next session. Collect the participant contact sheets.

Session 2:
Who Is Jesus, and Why Should I Care?

Jesus Christ

INTRODUCTION

Through the story of the woman at the well, we discover that in the midst of our searching, God through Jesus Christ is searching for us.

PREPARATION

Prepare yourself spiritually. Pray for yourself and for all the participants.

Review these director's notes.

Read Chapter 2 in *Beginnings: Along the Way: A Participant's Companion.*

Watch the video/DVD presentation.

Prepare the gathering space.

Prepare the small-group areas with extra copies of *Beginnings: Participant's Guide*, pencils/pens, and Bibles.

Check the TV and the VCR/DVD player, and cue the video/DVD.

Make sure nametags are out and direction signs are up.

Prepare for possible singing, and check the sound system.

Review the names of everyone. Call as many people as possible by their first name.

Pass out the contact forms to small-group leaders.

SERVE THE MEAL

WELCOME (5 minutes by director)

Welcome all participants.

Introduce the members of the leadership team.

Ask people to introduce themselves further at their snack/dinner/lunch table to other persons in their small group.

Share any housekeeping details.

State the focus of this session: "Today, through the story of a woman completing her daily tasks, we discover that in the midst of our searching, God through Jesus Christ is searching for us. You may read the story of this woman in your *Participant's Guide*" [or you, the director, may read John 4:3-29 aloud for everyone to hear].

SINGING
(optional; 5 minutes by music/worship leader)

VIDEO/DVD PRESENTATION 2 *(20 minutes)*

Start the video/DVD on time.

DISCUSSION *(45 minutes by small-group leader)*

Greet each member of the small group.

Pass around the contact form for the last time; it will be used only under special circumstances. At the end of the session, give it to the director.

Remind everyone about confidentiality. What is said within the small group should stay within the small group.

Group Questions

When you were a child, how did you answer the question, "What do you want to be when you grow up?" How accurate was your prediction?

Who do you think Jesus is? What names or titles do you use for Jesus: teacher, healer, social activist, magician, messiah, religious fanatic, mystic, hopeless romantic, enlightenment philosopher, hoax, compassionate friend, martyr? Why?

Imagine you are sitting on a park bench and Jesus comes and sits beside you. What would you do?

— Keep reading the paper and hope he does not notice you.
— Try to strike up a conversation. What would your opening line be?
— Ask for a favor. What would you ask for?
— Ask his advice. What would you want to know?
— What reaction would you expect from Jesus?

Take a moment and pair up with another person in your group. Ask each other: "What brings you to the well?"

What are you thirsty for?

Personal Questions

Can you see yourself as the woman at the well, looking for water and being found by Jesus? How do you think the people in her town responded when she told them about her conversation with Jesus?

What are you seeking?

CLOSING (*5 minutes by small-group leader*)

Remind everyone about the schedule for next week, and make other necessary announcements.

Invite the participants to pause for a minute of silence to reflect on this session.

Pray together.

Adjourn on time.

The director collects the contact forms one last time.

Session 3:
Why Am I Not Where I Want to Be?

Augustine — Missed Placed Loves
Self, Things, Others — that was meant
for God

Sin and the Cross — ways to Get Off Track

Pauls - "What I want to do, I don't
what I don't want to do, I do"

1) Pursue Things
2) Living into someone else's expectations
3) Pursue Self-sufficiency

INTRODUCTION

Through the tax collector Zacchaeus, we discover that when our lives seem to be falling apart, Jesus comes to us.

PREPARATION

Prepare yourself spiritually. Pray for yourself and for all the participants.

Review these director's notes.

Read Chapter 3 in *Beginnings: Along the Way: A Participant's Companion.*

Watch the video/DVD presentation.

Prepare the gathering space.

Prepare the small-group areas.

Check the TV and the VCR/DVD player, and cue the video/DVD.

Make sure nametags are out and direction signs are up.

Prepare for singing, and check the sound system.

SERVE THE MEAL

WELCOME (*5 minutes by director*)

Welcome all participants.

Share any housekeeping details.

State the focus of this session: "Today, we will hear the story of Zacchaeus, a tax collector, who was discovered by Jesus in a tree. You may read this story in your *Participant's Guide*" [or you, the director, may read Luke 19:1-10 aloud for everyone to hear].

SINGING

(*optional; 5 minutes by music/worship leader*)

VIDEO/DVD PRESENTATION 3 (*20 minutes*)

Start the video/DVD on time.

DISCUSSION (*45 minutes by small-group leader*)

Greet each member of the small group.

Group Questions

Have you ever had an experience like Rob's in which you felt in over your head or overwhelmed?

What are your top two choices in describing human nature:

_____selfish

_____good

_____naïve

_____evil

_____generous

_____innocent

_____clueless

_____other

Why did you make those choices?

Take a moment and pair up with another person in your group (different from the person you paired up with last week), and ask each other: "Where do you want to be? Why are you not there? How do you get there?"

Personal Questions

Can you identify with Zacchaeus watching for Jesus, with the crowd who observed their conversation, or with Jesus' friends who observed them? How do you think people responded when Zacchaeus showed up on their doorstep paying back everything he had stolen?

What are your dreams for your life? What is holding you back from achieving them?

Are you where you want to be in your life? If not, what is really keeping you from being where you want to be in your life?

Describe a situation in which one wrong deed led to another.

CLOSING *(5 minutes by small-group leader)*

Remind everyone about the schedule for next week, and make other necessary announcements.

Invite the participants to pause for a minute of silence to reflect on this session.

Pray together.

Adjourn on time.

Session 4:
What Happens When I Die?

Death and the Resurrection

INTRODUCTION

Through the story of two people on the day after the crucifixion, we discover that the resurrection of Jesus Christ is God's answer to the problem of death.

PREPARATION

Prepare yourself spiritually. Pray for yourself and for all the participants.

Review these director's notes.

Read Chapter 4 in *Beginnings: Along the Way: A Participant's Companion.*

Watch the video/DVD presentation.

Prepare the gathering space.

Prepare the small-group areas.

Check the TV and the VCR/DVD player, and cue the video/DVD.

Make sure nametags are out and direction signs are up.

Prepare for singing, and check the sound system.

SPECIAL NOTE

Decide if an additional training session is needed to prepare for the Day Apart retreat. Communicate your decision about this to the members of your leadership team.

SERVE THE MEAL

WELCOME *(5 minutes by director)*

Welcome all participants.

Share any housekeeping details.

Begin to promote the Day Apart retreat if this is your model.

State the focus of this session: "Today, Jesus has a conversation with two friends on the day of his resurrection from the dead. You may read this story in your *Participant's Guide*" [or you, the director, may read Luke 24:13-35 aloud for everyone to hear].

SINGING
(optional; 5 minutes by music/worship leader)

VIDEO/DVD PRESENTATION 4 *(20 minutes)*

Start the video/DVD on time.

DISCUSSION *(45 minutes by small-group leader)*

Greet each member of the small group.

Group Questions

Reporters from a British newspaper frequently ask celebrities, "How would you like to die?" Suppose a reporter has just arrived at your home and has asked you this question. How would you answer?

Name a person close to you who has died. What was your reaction?

Have you had an experience in your life that brought you to the point where you felt like you had been given a second life?

What do you believe happens when you die? In what way, if any, does your response make a difference in the way you live today?

Personal Questions

Recall your answer to the group question about the person close to you who died. What other thoughts or feelings do you have about the death of that person?

Imagine yourself walking along with the couple on the road to Emmaus, or imagine yourself with the friends back in Jerusalem who heard their story. What insights do you gain from them?

If you could write your own obituary, what would you say? What have you accomplished in your life? What has been left undone? If you have time, you may wish to write out your own obituary.

CLOSING *(5 minutes by small-group leader)*

Remind everyone about the schedule for next week, and make other necessary announcements.

Invite the participants to pause for a minute of silence to reflect on this session.

Pray together.

Adjourn on time.

Session 5:
Can I Trust God?

Providence and Suffering

INTRODUCTION

Can we trust God when our lives and world seem to be in chaos? Through the story of Moses, we are reminded that God has a plan that has existed from the beginning of creation for everyone to be in relationship with God.

PREPARATION

Prepare yourself spiritually. Pray for yourself and for all the participants.

Review these director's notes.

Read Chapter 5 in *Beginnings: Along the Way: A Participant's Companion.*

Watch the video/DVD presentation.

Prepare the gathering space.

Prepare the small-group areas.

Check the TV and the VCR/DVD player, and cue the video/DVD.

Make sure nametags are out and direction signs are up.

Prepare for singing, and check the sound system.

Review names of participants.

SERVE THE MEAL

WELCOME *(5 minutes by director)*

Welcome all participants.

Share any housekeeping details.

State the focus of this session: "Today, through Moses and God's people Israel, we will discover that God has a plan for our lives and for all of creation. You may read this story in your *Participant's Guide*" [or you, the director, may read Exodus 3:1-15 aloud for everyone to hear].

SINGING
(optional; 5 minutes by music/worship leader)

VIDEO/DVD PRESENTATION 5 *(20 minutes)*

Start the video/DVD on time.

DISCUSSION *(45 minutes by small-group leader)*

Greet each member of the small group.

Group Questions

Who are the people in your life who influenced your idea of God the most? Was their influence positive or negative? In what ways?

How did you picture God when you were a child?

_____ a gentle grandfather with a long white beard or grandmother in a rocking chair

_____ a stern judge in a black robe

_____ a bored spectator watching from a distance

_____ other

_____ I never thought about God when I was growing up.

How has your view of God changed? In what ways has it remained the same?

When things get really tough, who is the one person you can really trust?

When people say, "Trust God," what is your reaction?

Personal Questions

Moses was startled by a burning bush. Have you ever had such an experience? If so, what were the circumstances? What do you think Moses' wife and family said when he got home and told about his experience?

Have you ever had an experience that made you ask, "Where is God?" If so, what was it?

When have you had an experience when God came up and got right in your face? What was happening in your life both before and after that experience?

Do you find it hard to trust God with the things that are most important to you? Why or why not?

What would your ideal parent look like? What difference would it make in your life if you began to see God this way?

What does it mean to trust God in a world that has experienced the Jewish Holocaust, global terrorism, child abuse, poverty, and children being born with birth defects?

CLOSING *(5 minutes by small-group leader)*

Remind everyone about the schedule for next week, and make other necessary announcements.

Invite the participants to pause for a minute of silence to reflect on this session.

Pray together.

Adjourn on time.

SPECIAL NOTE

Begin to promote the Day Apart retreat and to register people for it if you are using the nine-week model.

Session 6:
How Does God Speak to Me?

The Bible

INTRODUCTION

When an Ethiopian official was looking for answers, he turned to the Scriptures for direction in his relationship with God.

PREPARATION

Prepare yourself spiritually. Pray for yourself and for all the participants.

Review these director's notes.

Read Chapter 6 in *Beginnings: Along the Way: A Participant's Companion.*

Watch the video/DVD presentation.

Prepare the gathering space.

Prepare the small-group areas.

Check the TV and the VCR/DVD player, and cue the video/DVD.

Make sure nametags are out and direction signs are up.

Prepare for singing, and check the sound system.

SPECIAL NOTE

Make sure that extra Bibles are available.

SERVE THE MEAL

WELCOME *(5 minutes by director)*

Welcome all participants.

Share any housekeeping details.

Give detailed information about the Day Apart retreat, and pass around the sign-up sheet (see page 62).

State the focus of this session: "Today, through an African official, we hear that the Bible gives Christians direction in our relationship with God. You may read this story in your *Participant's Guide*" [or you, the director, may read Acts 8:26-39 aloud for everyone to hear].

SINGING
(optional; 5 minutes by music/worship leader)

VIDEO/DVD PRESENTATION 6 *(20 minutes)*

Start the video/DVD on time.

DISCUSSION *(45 minutes by small-group leader)*

Greet each member of the small group.

Group Questions

If you own a Bible, when did you receive it?

What has been your experience when reading the Bible? (Check all that apply.)

_____ My mind wanders.

_____ It's boring.

_____ I don't understand the words or context.

_____ I discover people like me.

_____ I'm intimidated.

_____ God spoke directly to me.

Name some ways other than the Bible in which God speaks.

How do you respond to Rob's descriptions of the Bible as an oracle, charm, rulebook, confirmation of beliefs held, or as a road map or guide?

What did you hear from Rob that connects with your life?

Personal Questions

The Ethiopian official was looking for answers and needed some help. When have you felt this way? When have you helped someone else in this same situation?

Has God ever spoken to you? If so, how? What did God say?

Have you had an occasion when you read the Bible for instruction, direction, or help? If so, when? Why? What did you discover?

If you have a favorite Bible story, what is it? Why is it important to you?

Read from the New Testament a story when Jesus fed 4,000 people, Mark 8:1-10. Practice interpreting the Bible: What is this story about? How does this story connect with you? What does the story expect from you?

Read also from the New Testament a story about a sower throwing out some seed, Mark 4:1-8. Practice interpreting the Bible: What is this story about? How does this story connect with you? What does the story expect from you? After you have thought about the story, read Mark 4:13-20 for Jesus' interpreta-

tion of the story. How does Jesus' interpretation change how you understand the story.

If you are really adventurous, try reading the entire New Testament book of Mark. Doing so takes about one hour and covers the whole of Jesus' life from his baptism in the river Jordan to his resurrection in Jerusalem.

CLOSING (*5 minutes by small-group leader*)

Remind everyone about the schedule for the Day Apart retreat (if you are following the nine-week option) sand for next week's session. Also make other necessary announcements.

Continue registering for the Day Apart retreat.

Invite the participants to pause for a minute of silence to reflect on this session.

Pray together.

Adjourn on time.

SPECIAL NOTE

Day Apart registration forms are turned in to the director.

The Day Apart Retreat

The Day Apart retreat is crucial to the nine-week model of *Beginnings*. This day focuses on the issue of helping all inquirers claim Jesus Christ as the guide of their lives. As people gather together, share several meals and snacks, go for walks, and participate in a worship service that may include Holy Communion, friendships are cemented in ways not possible at a weekly session. In this relaxed environment, people unwind and barriers begin to fall. The day is usually a Saturday, Sunday, or holiday. The sessions for this day are three presentations on salvation and conversion, forgiveness and wholeness, and prayer. As in the rest of *Beginnings*, your congregation's guests should not be expected to pay for this retreat day.

When your use the twelve-week model of *Beginnings*, these three sessions are simply additional days. This model is especially useful when a number of participants cannot be away for a full day. People's lives can be complex, and a day away simply is not possible for them. Yet, these three sessions are at the heart of the program and should not be dropped. The session notes that follow assume a Day Apart, but you may also choose to run each session just like the previous six.

A possible timetable for the Day Apart retreat is as follows:

8:00 AM	Leaders and Helpers Arrive and Set Out Breakfast Snacks
8:30 AM	Participants Arrive
9:00 AM	Introduction to the Day and Gathering Songs (optional)
9:20 AM	Video/DVD Presentation 7: If I Don't Feel Lost, Why Do I Need to Be Found? Salvation and Conversion
9:40 AM	Refreshment Break
10:00 AM	Discussion
10:50 AM	Break
11:00 AM	Introduction to Video/DVD Presentation 8
11:05 AM	Video/DVD Presentation 8: Can I Start Again? Forgiveness and Wholeness
11:25 AM	Discussion
12:00 noon	Break
12:15 PM	Lunch and Continuing Group Discussion
1:00 PM	Free Time for Walk or Conversations
1:30 PM	Introduction to Video/DVD Presentation 9
1:35 PM	Video/DVD Presentation 9: How Do I Speak to God? Prayer
1:50 PM	Discussion
2:30 PM	Break
2:45 PM	Large-Group Worship (Possibly Including Holy Communion)
3:45 PM	Adjourn

DAY APART ORGANIZATION

The Day Apart may be planned by you as director (or by the team coordinator in larger programs) along with the rest of the members of your leadership team. Your meal coordinator and music/worship leader will have major roles to play on this day. There are a number of particular, new responsibilities for this retreat.

We recommend holding your Day Apart away from the location of your weekly sessions, perhaps in a nearby local congregation, campground, vacation house, or retreat facility. Another congregation that is also conducting *Beginnings* might exchange facilities with you for the day. The advantage of a new location is that people will focus on one another and the presentations in a fresh way.

If you use a different location, coordinate with the site's staff about special foods you require, a public address system, a TV and a VCR/DVD player, a chalkboard/whiteboard for announcements, childcare space, and sufficient places for your small groups to meet. Arrange for someone to look after any children participants need to bring with them. Because of the significance of this day, it is best that the children who come are occupied fully throughout the day and do not come in and out of the adult gatherings. Have a full, fun day for the children so that their parents can relax and engage in deep, meaningful conversations. If necessary, remember to take transparencies/slides/computer-generated video slides and projectors; and remind participants to bring their copy of *Beginnings: A Participant's Guide* and a Bible. Also take Bibles and books for participants who might have left theirs at home.

Each small-group member should fill in a registration form (see page 62), which should be circulated beginning in Week 6, for the Day Apart retreat. Include on the form details of the date, costs, and other arrangements. Ask for information regarding special diets and childcare needs. Make sure everyone has a map and a schedule for the day.

A significant part of the day is the possible inclusion of a closing worship service. The service should offer a joyful experience in music, Scripture, prayer, and opportunities for participants to tell about significant insights or experiences they had during the Day Apart or during earlier sessions of the *Beginnings* program. A model for a closing order of worship based upon Luke 24:13-32 is included in the instructions for Session 9 (see page 100). The worship may include Holy Communion if you have ordained clergy present at the Day Apart retreat. In some traditions, everyone who wants to be in communion with Jesus Christ and the gathered community may share the Holy Meal. In other traditions, only baptized members may share the Holy Meal. Decide about whether or not to include Holy Communion during the closing worship according to what is most appropriate in your tradition and for your *Beginnings* group.

At the end of the day, some people will have obligations that will require that they leave after the closing worship. If persons are able, however, make plans to have a meal at the site or make reservations at a local restaurant for your participants who wish to continue the fellowship.

SAMPLE DAY APART REGISTRATION FORM

We will be gathering on Saturday, October 18, for our "Day Apart" Retreat. We will gather at the Shalom Center at 100 W. Trade Street at 8:30 AM and continue until 3:45 PM. We will begin with a light breakfast. Lunch will be served. Childcare will be offered throughout the day on site. On this day, we will cover three of the most important sessions of *Beginnings*. This is a day not to miss. Below is the schedule for the day. Please fill out this registration form as soon as possible, and give it to your small-group leader. A map for the site is on the back of this form.

Put schedule here:

Registration:

Name:
Childcare: Yes__   No__
Ages/Names of children:
Special Diet Requirements:
Would you be interested in supper on this day?

(Map on reverse side)

Session 7 (Day Apart 1):
If I Don't Feel Lost,
Why Do I Need to Be Found?

Salvation and Conversion

Note: *If you are not having a Day Apart retreat, conduct this session in the same way as the previous six sessions.*

INTRODUCTION

Through the story of a runaway son, we hear that God invites each of us on a lifelong journey during which our relationship with God deepens.

PREPARATION

Make sure everyone has a copy of the schedule for the day (see page 93 for outline).

Prepare yourself spiritually. Pray for yourself and for all the participants.

Review these director's notes for all three sessions.

Read Chapters 7, 8, and 9 in *Beginnings: Along the Way: A Participant's Companion.*

Watch the three video/DVD presentations.

Prepare the gathering space.

Check the TV and the VCR/DVD player, and cue the video/DVD.

Prepare the chairs for small groups, and put out pencils/pens.

Bring plate and cup, along with bread and grape juice/wine, if you are having Holy Communion as part of your closing worship service for the Day Apart retreat.

Make sure nametags are out and direction signs are up.

Prepare for singing, and check the sound system.

Be on site at least thirty minutes before participants arrive.

ARRIVAL AND BREAKFAST SNACKS
(30 minutes)

Set out morning/breakfast snacks (not a full breakfast buffet), drinks (include caffeinated and decaffeinated beverages), welcome participants, and visit.

WELCOME *(10 minutes by director)*

Welcome all participants.

Share any housekeeping details.

State the focus of this session: "This session will tell the story of a runaway son who eventually comes home, reminding us that God invites each of us on a lifelong journey during which our relationship with God deepens. You may read this story in your *Participant's Guide*" [or you, the director, may read Luke 15:11-24 aloud for everyone to hear].

SINGING
(optional; 10-12 minutes by music/worship leader)

VIDEO/DVD PRESENTATION 7 *(20 minutes)*

Start the video/DVD on time.

BREAK *(20 minutes)*

DISCUSSION *(50 minutes by small-group leader)*

Group Questions

Recall a time when you returned to your hometown or old school or some other place after a long absence. How did it feel? In what ways was it awkward? In what ways was it comforting? Why?

Has there been a time in your life when you felt like the younger son or like the waiting father or like the older brother who stayed behind? If so, what were the circumstances? Why did you feel that way?

Has anyone ever approached you about God in a way that turned you off? On the other hand, have you ever had an experience that ignited a spark to seek God more earnestly? If so, what was it?

At this point in your spiritual journey, where are you in your relationship with God?

Personal Questions

Take some time for the following exercise: Draw a chart of your own personal spiritual journey. Use a single line that represents your relationship to God. At each valley, peak, gentle hill, or plateau, write down the event, person, or experience that was involved.

Do you feel lost or found or just comfortable in your spiritual journey? Why?

CLOSING [of First Day Apart Session]
(5 minutes by small-group leader)

Remind everyone about the break and the schedule for the rest of the day (if you are having the Day Apart retreat).

Invite the participants to pause for a minute of silence to reflect on this session.

Pray together.

Adjourn on time.

SHORT BREAK (10 minutes)

Session 8 (Day Apart 2): Can I Start Again?

Forgiveness and Wholeness

Note: If you are not having a Day Apart retreat, conduct this session in the same way as the previous sessions.

INTRODUCTION

Through two stories we hear that a relationship with Jesus opens for us the possibilities of being forgiven and forgiving other people and finding wholeness in body, mind, spirit, and relationships.

PREPARATION

Check out again and clean up the gathering space.
Check the TV and the VCR/DVD player, and cue the video/DVD.

WELCOME *(3 minutes by director)*

State the focus of this session: "This session will focus on two stories—of a woman being forgiven and a woman being healed—reminding us that a relationship with Jesus opens for us the possibilities of being forgiven and forgiving other people and finding wholeness in body, mind, spirit, and relationships. You may read these stories in your *Participant's Guide*" [or you, the director, may read John 8:2-11 and Mark 5:24b-29 aloud for everyone to hear].

VIDEO/DVD PRESENTATION 8 *(20 minutes)*

Start the video/DVD on time.

DISCUSSION *(35 minutes by small-group leader)*

Group Questions

Have you ever known anyone who changed completely? How or why did it happen? Did you like the person better before or after the change?

Name someone close to you who needs forgiveness in his or her life. Why does this person need forgiveness?

Name someone close to you who needs healing in her or his life. Why does this person need healing?

Can you identify with the biblical woman in trouble or with the crowd ready to stone her or with the bleeding woman? Why or why not?

Personal Questions

What area in your life needs forgiveness?

Is God nudging you to forgive someone or to restore a broken relationship?

What area in your life needs healing?

If you could start your life over from this point on, with no baggage and no past, what would your life look like?

CLOSING *[of Second Day Apart Session]* *(5 minutes by small-group leader)*

Remind everyone about the break and about the schedule for the rest of the day (if you are having the Day Apart retreat).

Invite the participants to pause for a minute of silence to reflect on this session.

Pray together.

Adjourn on time.

DAY APART SHORT BREAK BEFORE LUNCH *(15 minutes)*

DAY APART LUNCH AND FREE TIME *(1 hour and 15 minutes)*

Session 9 (Day Apart 3): How Do I Speak to God?

Prayer

Note: If you are not having a Day Apart retreat, conduct this session in the same way as the previous sessions.

INTRODUCTION

Jesus teaches us that prayer is speaking and listening to God.

PREPARATION

Check out again and clean up the gathering space.
Check the TV and the VCR/DVD player, and cue the video/DVD.

WELCOME *(5 minutes by director)*

Share any final housekeeping details.
State the focus of this session: "This session will focus on Jesus teaching us how to speak and listen to God through prayer. You may read this story in your *Participant's Guide*" [or you, the director, may read Luke 11:1-13 aloud for everyone to hear].

VIDEO/DVD PRESENTATION 9 *(20 minutes)*

Start the video/DVD on time.

DISCUSSION *(40 minutes by small-group leader)*

Group Questions

How often do you speak with your best friend? Is this often enough? What keeps you from talking more often?
Read The Lord's Prayer aloud as a group. What is it saying?
Rob described prayer as "drawing near to God," an experience that can happen through words, wood, or life. Can you name a time when you prayed to God without using any words? If so, what were the circumstances?

If you had the opportunity to talk with God alone and uninterrupted, what would be one of the first things you would say?

Personal Questions

The disciples asked Jesus how to pray. Why do you think they asked Jesus this question?
When you pray, do you think God is listening? Why do you think that?
Have any of your prayers been answered? Do you have any idea why?
Have any of your prayers gone unanswered? Do you have any idea why?

Write down some prayer requests for:

____ yourself
____ your family
____ your friends
____ your community
____ our nation
____ the world

Pray for someone you dislike: an ex-spouse, an ex-friend, a former boss, an estranged family member.
Read Matthew 6:5-13. What does Jesus tell us about prayer? What does this message tell you about how to pray? Will you pray any differently having heard this message? Why or why not?
Consider praying The Lord's Prayer each day in the coming week.

CLOSING [of Third Day Apart Session]
(10 minutes by small-group leader)

Remind everyone about the day's final schedule and the schedule for next week. Also make other necessary announcements.

Begin to promote the Love Feast closing celebration (Session 12).

See if people are available for supper after the end of the day's sessions.

Invite the participants to pause for a minute of silence to reflect on the session.

Pray together about the whole day's experience.

Adjourn on time for a break and (optional) to prepare for Holy Communion.

SPECIAL NOTE

Begin to advertise for the closing Love Feast at this time. Use the invitation and the registration form found on page 63.

CLOSING WORSHIP (optional at Day Apart; 60 minutes by pastor)

Plan a worship experience that provides music, Scripture, and opportunities for participants to talk to one another about significant or meaningful insights gained during the day. The director and music/worship leader should work together to integrate the music carefully with the Scripture and the gathered participants. Use the following model to plan the worship:

Joyful songs or hymns of praise
An invitation for participants to share their joys with the entire group
A prayer of gratitude
Scripture: Luke 24:13-32. The Road to Emmaus
A brief reflection or sermon on Luke 25:13-32 (5 minutes)
Testimonies from participants about ways they have recognized Jesus Christ during the Day Apart (or other times)
Joyful songs or hymns of praise
Closing prayer: Get in a circle, hold hands, and offer a final dismissal with blessing.

If an ordained clergyperson is available, you may choose to offer Holy Communion before the closing circle prayer.

ADJOURN FOR HOME OR SUPPER WITH OTHER PARTICIPANTS

Session 10:
How Can I Make a Life
and Not Just a Living?

The Good Life

INTRODUCTION

Following Jesus Christ demands a different way of living that focuses on loving God and loving other people.

PREPARATION

Prepare yourself spiritually. Pray for yourself and for all the participants.

Review these director's notes.

Read Chapter 10 in *Beginnings: Along The Way: A Participant's Companion.*

Watch the video/DVD presentation.

Prepare the gathering space and small-group areas.

Check the TV and the VCR/DVD player, and cue the video/DVD.

Make sure nametags are out and direction signs are up.

Prepare for singing, and check the sound system.

SPECIAL NOTE

Pass out registration sheets for the closing Love Feast and invitations to it (see page 63).

WELCOME *(5 minutes by director)*

Welcome all participants.

Share any housekeeping details.

State the focus of this session: "Today, we overhear a conversation between a man and Jesus about how to live a good life, by loving God and other people. You may read this story in your *Participant's Guide*" [or you, the director, may read Luke 18:18-23 aloud for everyone to hear].

SINGING
(optional; 10 minutes by music/worship leader)

VIDEO/DVD PRESENTATION 10 *(20 minutes)*

Start the video/DVD on time.

DISCUSSION *(45 minutes by small-group leader)*

Greet each member of the small group.

Group Questions

Divide your small group into two teams. The first team will advocate "the good life" as defined by people in your grandparents' generation. The second team will advocate "the good life" as defined by your own generation. At the end of the debate, discuss which generation is more or less satisfied by their answers.

Who or what is in control of your life now?

_____ to-do list
_____ your PDA
_____ your e-mail inbox
_____ your children
_____ your employer
_____ your 401K or pension plan
_____ an ex-friend
_____ your career
_____ your money and possessions
_____ God

How do you respond to Rob's statement, "We are seeking to fill our lives with other things rather than the one thing that was made to fulfill us."

Who has modeled an authentic, joyful life for you? What makes this person special?

Personal Questions

Think about your favorite fantasies as a child. What roles did you play? Someone's hero? Someone's beauty? Having a particular profession? How relevant do these fantasies seem to your life now? If you could adopt a new role for your life, what would it be?

What is the primary thing/commandment/law/goal in your life? Does your primary thing/commandment/law/goal seem consistent with God's commandment/law/goal for you?

What are some qualities that you believe are fundamental to a good life?

Do you make a living, or do you have a life?

CLOSING (*7 minutes by small-group leader*)

Remind everyone about the schedule for next week, and make other necessary announcements.

Invite the participants to pause for a minute of silence to reflect on this session.

Pray together.

Adjourn on time.

SPECIAL NOTES

Promote the closing Love Feast, especially inviting family and friends to come and participate. Pass around registration forms for the Love Feast, and distribute invitations to give to friends.

Tell participants that at the next session (11), each participant will be asked to speak about each other person in the group and to name one gift each person possesses. For example, someone may say, "John has the gift of compassion." or "Susan has the gift of honesty." Ask the participants to think about one another and one another's gifts in the week ahead. If they believe that they will be uncomfortable sharing orally, they may choose simply to write something down for each person and be ready to hand it to the person next week. More information is provided in the *Beginnings: Participant's Guide*.

Session 11:
Why Should I Join Any Group That Will Have Me as a Member?

Church Membership

INTRODUCTION

Based on an illustration about the human body, we discover that following Jesus Christ includes being a part of a church community.

PREPARATION

Prepare yourself spiritually. Pray for yourself and for all the participants.

Review these director's notes.

Read Chapter 11 in *Beginnings: Along the Way: A Participant's Companion.*

Watch the video/DVD presentation.

Prepare the gathering space and the small-group areas.

Check the TV and the VCR/DVD player, and cue the video/DVD.

Make sure nametags are out and direction signs are up.

Prepare for singing, and check the sound system.

SPECIAL NOTE

Make copies of the questionnaires (see page 64) for participants and leaders and distribute prior to breaking into small groups.

WELCOME *(3 minutes by director)*

Welcome all participants.

Share any housekeeping details.

State the focus of this session: "Using an illustration about the human body, we discover that following Jesus Christ includes being a part of a church community. You may read this story in your *Participant's Guide*" [or you, the director, may read 1 Corinthians 12:4-27 aloud for everyone to hear].

SINGING
(optional; 10 minutes by music/worship leader)

VIDEO/DVD PRESENTATION 11 *(20 minutes)*

Start the video/DVD on time.

DISCUSSION *(45 minutes by small-group leader)*

SPECIAL NOTE

Begin this time of sharing by asking all participants to share with the other persons in their group the spiritual gifts they see in one another. They may do so orally or in written form on slips of paper. This is a time to affirm the God-given gifts and fruits of the Spirit that each person has. The small-group leader should speak last, to give everyone else the chance to speak first.

Group Questions

Name the part of the human body that best describes you. Why?

Go around the circle and share with one another the gifts you assigned each person (see the end of last week's session for details).

With what group/sports team/ethnic group/hobby/interest do you identify?

When someone says to you, "Let's go to church!" what image or feeling first comes to your mind?

Personal Questions

What is the one place in the world that you would most like to visit? Imagine you have just won four free tickets to go there. Whom would you take with you? Why did you ask these people? What does this choice of this place and these people say about you?

Name the people in your life who have really taken the time to get to know you. How did they show you that they care? Do you have more or fewer of these people in your life as the years go by?

Have you ever been in a church where you felt the presence of God? If so, what was it like?

What would it be like for you to be a part of a community that cares for the outcast?

Can you see yourself as part of such a community? Why or why not?

Having experienced *Beginnings*, are you more likely to give a congregation a chance? Why?

CLOSING *(5 minutes by small-group leader)*

Remind everyone about the schedule for next week, and make other necessary announcements.

Invite the participants to pause for a minute of silence to reflect on this session.

Adjourn on time.

SPECIAL NOTES

Continue to register people for the Love Feast, encouraging family and friends to come by using the Love Feast invitations. Pass out the invitations. Register people.

Turn in the Love Feast registration forms to the meal coordinator.

Pass out the final participant questionnaires (see page 64), and ask participants to fill them out before they leave.

Small-group leaders should take home and fill out their survey/questionnaire (see page 66) about each person in their group.

Also, each small-group leader should take home and fill out his or her own evaluation of the program (see page 65).

Session 12:
Love Feast!

Remembering, Sharing, and Continuing the Journey

INTRODUCTION

We encourage everyone to remember the experiences they have had during *Beginnings* and to celebrate what each participant has discovered about God.

THE LOVE FEAST

Like a school graduation, the Love Feast is both an ending and a beginning. The purpose of the love feast is to conclude the *Beginnings* program and to encourage those who attended to invite other people to the next program. The title, Love Feast or Agape Meal, recalls the meals that Jesus shared with his disciples during his ministry and expresses the fellowship and community sharing enjoyed by the family of Christ. While the origin of the Love Feast is closely associated with the origins of the Lord's Supper in the New Testament, it is not a sacramental meal. Traditionally practiced by Moravians and Methodists worldwide, it tends to be a more informal meal in which testimonies, prayers, and thanksgivings by participants are the focus. [See *The United Methodist Book of Worship*, pages 581–84 for more details.]

A prayer for blessing this meal is an old verse written by John Cenick:

Be present at our table, Lord;
   be here and everywhere adored;
Thy creatures bless, and grant that we
   may feast in paradise with Thee.

Begin talking about the final Love Feast during the Day Apart retreat. At the Day Apart or in Week 10 of the 12-week model, advertise the Love Feast and distribute invitations. Try to determine how many persons will be coming and turn in the count to your meal coordinator.

SAMPLE INVITATION

Beginnings: An Introduction to Christian Faith
We invite you to our final celebration and Love Feast.
November 5th
at Central United Methodist Church.
The time is from 5:30 PM to 8:00 PM. The Love Feast includes a meal, singing, a brief presentation, and a time for our participants to share their spiritual journey over the past weeks. Free childcare is available.

The meal and program are offered without cost to guests.

SCHEDULE

The Love Feast schedule is similar to but different from every other session:

5:00 PM	Leaders Meet to Prepare and Pray
5:15 PM	Participants and Guests Begin to Arrive
5:30 PM	Supper
6:15 PM	Welcome by Director
6:20 PM	Worship Led by Worship Leader
6:35 PM	Video/DVD Presentation 12
6:55 PM	Director Talk
7:05 PM	Remembering and Sharing
7:50 PM	Closing and Prayer
8:00 PM	Adjourn

The meal at the Love Feast should be the most festive meal of the program. Your meal coordinator may contract with a caterer to provide the meal, while a covered-dish supper is another possibility. A range of good desserts (including some that are sugar free), good coffees and teas (including decaffeinated or herbal beverages), and dessert mints encourages everyone to stay a little longer. Make sure the tables are decorated and a festive atmosphere prevails.

A critical aspect of this event is that all your participants are encouraged to invite family members, friends, neighbors, and coworkers who have not been participating in the program, especially persons who are not active in a community of faith. Older children, including those of first-time guests, should be encouraged to come and attend the group sessions. A nursery may be provided for the younger children. As the participants share their new knowledge and experiences, their friends will begin to see how other people are on the way with Jesus Christ. Many future *Beginnings* participants will come from first-time guests at your Love Feast.

On the night of the Love Feast, invite everyone to arrive at 5:30 PM and share the meal together. The director offers a simple grace before the meal. At 6:15 PM, the director welcomes everyone. This may also be the appropriate time to thank those people who have organized your entire *Beginnings* program and especially the preparation for this evening. If your music/worship leader desires, the singing may start at 6:20 PM and be energetic and Christ-centered.

After watching the final video/DVD presentation, the director or your pastor begins the evening with a short (no more than eight minutes) talk based on Paul's experience in Athens when he arrived to proclaim the gospel (Acts 17:32-34). Paul discovered that there were three reactions to his preaching. First, "some scoffed" (verse 32). Second, other Athenian listeners to Paul said, "We will hear you again" (verse 32). Suggest that people attend the next *Beginnings* program and invite a friend to come along. Have invitations and brochures for the next program available. Finally, as Paul preached, "some of the Athenians joined Paul" (verse 34). A gentle invitation to visit your local congregation may follow.

Faith sharing follows the director's witness. This time may include testimonies and praise. Testimonies may include a personal witness to God's grace over the course of the program or an account of what God has been doing in the lives of participants. Praise may take the form of hymns, songs, choruses, or spoken words of thanksgiving. Spontaneous prayers may also be part of the evening. The director guides this time, sometimes alternating music and testimonies, for as long as the Holy Spirit moves. The schedule provides adequate time for such sharing.

At 7:50 PM, the director closes the Love Feast by summarizing the evening and then closing with a prayer.

At the end of the sharing and testimonies, invite everyone to stay for coffee, dessert, and more conversation. Many people may stay and talk.

PREPARATION

Prepare yourself spiritually. Pray for yourself and for all the participants.

Review these director's notes.

Read Chapter 12 in *Beginnings: Along the Way: A Participant's Companion.*

Watch the video/DVD presentation.

Prepare the gathering space.

Check the TV and the VCR/DVD player, and cue the video/DVD.

Make sure nametags are out (You will need many extra ones for first-time guests.) and direction signs are up.

Put brochures for the next *Beginnings* program on the registration table.

Prepare for singing, and check the sound system.

SPECIAL NOTES

At the registration table, place a box or basket to collect the final questionnaires from participants.

Collect the host questionnaires and evaluations from your small-group leaders about each member in their group.

SERVE THE MEAL

Have cake, sweet bread, or cookies as a dessert. Save this part of the meal for the time of remembering and sharing.

WELCOME *(5 minutes by director)*

Welcome all participants, especially first-time guests. Introduce the members of your leadership team. Share any housekeeping details.

State the focus of this session: "Today, we want to enable everyone to remember their experiences in this program and to celebrate what each one of us has discovered about Jesus Christ. You may read a word from one of the Bible's poets in your *Participant's Guide*" [or you, the director, may read Psalm 77:11-12 aloud for everyone to hear].

SINGING

(optional; up to 15 minutes by music/worship leader)

VIDEO/DVD PRESENTATION 12 *(20 minutes)*

Start the video/DVD on time.

PRESENTATION *(10 minutes by director)*

After watching the final video/DVD presentation, the director continues with an eight-minute talk based on Paul's experience in Athens when he arrived to proclaim the gospel (Acts 17:32-34).

REMEMBERING AND SHARING .

(45 minutes guided by director)

Have a host or hostess bring a pitcher of water and a tray of desserts (Cake, sweet bread, or cookies are easy to handle.) to each table. The host or hostess will offer water and dessert to someone at the table. As the host or hostess offers these items, he or she will also offer the person some words of kindness. The person who receives the water, dessert, and words of kindness will, in turn, offer water, dessert, and words of kindness to the next person at the table. This process continues until water, dessert, and words of kindness have been passed around the entire table.

After this part of the Love Feast, invite participants to a time of faith sharing.

This faith sharing begins with the director giving her or his witness. This time of faith sharing may include testimonies and praise. Testimonies may include a personal witness to Jesus Christ's presence throughout the program or an account of what God has been doing in the lives of others. Praise may take the form of hymns, songs, choruses, or spoken words of thanksgiving. Spontaneous prayers may also be part of the evening. The director guides this time, sometimes alternating music and testimonies, for as long as the Holy Spirit moves.

Personal Questions

How have you experienced God over these past weeks? What has surprised you?

What have you discovered about yourself?

What are you going to do next?

Whom are you going to tell?

What is the biggest decision you are facing at this time in your life? To whom, if anyone, will you look for help in making this decision?

CLOSING *(10 minutes by director)*

Thank everyone for participating in *Beginnings*.

Pass around invitations and brochures about the next *Beginnings* program, and put additional copies on the registration table.

Remind people to put questionnaires and evaluations on the registration table.

Invite everyone to pause for a minute of silence to reflect on this session.

Led by the director, stand in a large circle, hold hands, and pray together.

Adjourn on time.

Notes

Notes

Notes